CO-PARENTING WITH A NARCISSISTIC EX 101

STEP BY STEP GUIDE TO SET AND MAINTAIN BOUNDARIES, PROTECT YOUR CHILDREN, MANAGE EMOTIONAL EXHAUSTION AND MOVE FORWARD WITH PEACE IN YOUR HEART

CASEY JORDAN

CONTENTS

Introduction — 7

CHAPTER 1 — 11
1.1 The Psychology Behind Narcissism — 12
1.2 Recognizing Narcissistic Behavior in Your Ex — 14
1.3 The Impact of Narcissism on Relationships — 17
1.4 Narcissistic Tactics and How They Manipulate — 19
1.5 The Difference Between Overt and Covert Narcissism — 23

2. MASTERING COMMUNICATION WITHOUT CONFLICT — 27
2.1 The Art of Gray Rock: Communicating Without Conflict — 29
2.2 Setting the Stage: Structured Communication Platforms — 39
2.3 Documenting Everything: The Importance of Written Records — 43
2.4 Deciphering Manipulative Messages: Reading Between the Lines — 46
2.5 The Power of Brevity: Keeping Communication Short and Sweet — 50

3. BOUNDARIES - THE BLUEPRINT FOR PEACE — 55
3.1 Identifying Non-Negotiable Boundaries — 56
3.2 Implementing Boundaries Without Escalation — 60
3.3 When Boundaries Are Crossed: Enforcement Strategies — 63
3.4 The Role of Legal Boundaries and Orders — 65
3.5 Teaching Your Children About Boundaries — 72

4. NURTURING EMOTIONAL SAFETY AND INTELLIGENCE — 77
4.1 Recognizing Signs of Emotional Manipulation in Children — 77
4.2 Fostering Open Communication with Your Children — 81

4.3 Strategies for Counteracting Parental Alienation	85
4.4 Building Resilience: Helping Your Children Bounce Back	88
4.5 The Importance of a Supportive Home Environment	91
5. PRIORITIZING PERSONAL PEACE: THE SELF-CARE BLUEPRINT	97
5.1 The Fundamentals of Self-Care	98
5.2 Emotional Self-Care: Healing from Narcissistic Abuse	104
5.3 Physical Self-Care: The Role of Exercise and Nutrition	115
5.4 Social Self-Care: Building a Support Network	118
5.5 Spiritual Self-Care: Finding Peace and Purpose	122
6. FINANCIAL INDEPENDENCE AND RECOVERY	127
6.1 Untangling Financial Ties With a Narcissist	127
6.2 Strategies for Financial Empowerment	133
6.3 Navigating Child Support and Alimony Challenges	136
6.4 Understanding Your Legal Rights in Co-Parenting	139
6.5 Preparing for Legal Battles: Documentation and Evidence	144
7. REDEFINING AND REBUILDING	147
7.1 Redefining Your Identity After Divorce	148
7.2 Setting Goals for a New Beginning	157
7.3 The Journey of Finding Happiness Again	160
7.4 Dating After Divorce: When and How	162
7.5 Crafting a Positive Legacy for Your Children	165
8. HIGH-STAKES CO-PARENTING	169
8.1 Navigating Smear Campaigns and Public Perception	170
8.2 Crisis Management: When to Seek Professional Help	173
8.3 Techniques for Emotional Detachment in Conflict	175
9. STEPPING INTO YOUR POWER	179
9.1 Building a Personal Empowerment Plan	180
9.2 Advocating for Your Children's Rights	184

9.3 Using Your Experience to Help Others   186
9.4 Establishing a Co-Parenting Advocacy Group   189
9.5 The Power of Storytelling: Sharing Your Journey 193

Conclusion   199
References   203

INTRODUCTION

Have you ever found yourself wondering if there's a light at the end of the tunnel when it comes to co-parenting with a narcissistic ex? If so, you're not alone. Many people navigate this challenging journey feeling overwhelmed by frustration, confusion, and a longing for solutions that seem just out of reach. It's a path marked by unique challenges that demand not just practical strategies, but also emotional resilience. Recognizing this complex interplay of needs is where our journey begins.

Imagine trying to steer a ship through a storm with someone who insists on controlling the wheel while disregarding the compass, and ignoring the seasoned advice of the crew. This scenario mirrors the complexities and challenges of co-parenting with a narcissist. The journey is unpredictable, fraught with power struggles and manipulation, and requires you to become adept at navigating these choppy waters to ensure the safety and well-being of your most precious cargo: your children.

Co-parenting with a narcissist is akin to playing a game where the rules constantly change but are never communicated. One day, your co-parenting arrangement might seem relatively smooth, and the next, you're blindsided by unreasonable demands or outright hostility. This inconsistency and unpredictability stems from the narcissist's need for control and admiration, which often leads to conflict and manipulation. These dynamics can create an environment of confusion and instability for children, who thrive on consistency and predictability.

This book is crafted as a comprehensive guide to co-parenting with a narcissistic ex, designed with a single purpose in mind: to empower you. It aims to equip you with the tools needed to set and maintain boundaries, protect your children, manage emotional exhaustion, and rebuild your life with happiness. This is not just a manual, it is a companion for those moments when the way forward seems clouded.

My motivation for writing this book is deeply personal. Without diving into specifics, I have a profound connection to the topic, having faced similar challenges myself. For years, I've dedicated my time to understanding the dynamics of narcissistic relationships, drawing from both personal experience and extensive research. I hold qualifications in counseling and family mediation, and I have spent over a decade studying the effects of narcissistic behavior in relationships, particularly in co-parenting situations. I've encountered countless stories of individuals navigating the same difficult terrain, and these encounters have shaped my deep empathy and expertise on the subject. I am fueled by a combination of this extensive research, and a heartfelt desire to offer support and solutions. This passion has been the driving force behind every page, ensuring that the insights and strategies shared are practical, empathetic, and effective.

As you turn the pages, you'll find that the book is structured to address key areas critical to successful co-parenting with a narcissistic ex. These include understanding the nature of narcissism, mastering effective communication techniques, setting and maintaining healthy boundaries, protecting and supporting your children through the process, prioritizing your own well-being, and navigating the intricacies of legal and financial independence. This book marries practical advice with emotional support, drawing on the latest research, expert insights, and real-life examples to offer a roadmap which is both empowering and actionable.

Written for anyone co-parenting with a narcissistic ex, including divorced or separated parents, and professionals working with such individuals, this book ensures that its content is relevant and accessible to a wide audience. It's my mission to provide you with the resources, strategies, and support needed to navigate this challenging journey successfully, making you feel understood and far from alone.

As we embark on this journey together, I want to leave you with a message of hope and empowerment. Despite the inherent challenges of co-parenting with a narcissistic ex, it is possible to manage the situation effectively, and to rebuild a life marked by happiness and fulfillment. Together, we'll explore the path to achieving just that, while ensuring that you emerge stronger, more knowledgeable, and with a renewed sense of purpose. Welcome to a guide that seeks not just to inform, but to transform.

1

In the realm of relationships and co-parenting, understanding the complex nature of narcissism is not just beneficial—it's vital. The term "narcissist" is frequently tossed around in casual conversations, often misused to label anyone who seems a bit too self-involved. However, the reality of narcissism, particularly when it comes to navigating a co-parenting relationship with a narcissist, is far more nuanced and challenging than mere self-absorption.

Narcissism runs deeper than selfish vanity, and a narcissist's self-obsession and preoccupation with their own needs often negatively impacts those around them. An example of this behavior, when a narcissist cares only about fulfilling their own wants and needs, is the rapper Kanye West's outburst at the 2009 VMAs. As Taylor Swift was accepting her award for best female video on stage, Kanye West took the microphone from her and announced that Beyoncé should have won the award instead. This act was not beneficial to Beyoncé, and completely ruined Taylor's special moment. Kanye wanted to give his opinion and so he did, with no regard for how his actions would affect others. This moment perfectly encapsulates the self-importance of a narcissist and is available to watch on YouTube and TikTok.

Now consider a scenario where during a parent-teacher conference, one parent monopolizes the conversation, turning every teacher's observation into a testament to their own excellence, whether in their parenting skills or their child's inherited traits. This behavior may raise eyebrows, but when understood through the lens of narcissism, it becomes a textbook example of the need for admiration—a hallmark of narcissistic personality disorder (NPD).

1.1 THE PSYCHOLOGY BEHIND NARCISSISM

Understanding the roots: Narcissism, especially in its most detrimental forms, doesn't sprout overnight. It's the fruit of a complex interplay between genetic predispositions and environmental factors. Research suggests that certain genetic traits may predispose individuals to NPD, but these traits need environmental triggers to fully develop into narcissism. Early childhood experiences, such as excessive pampering by parents or, conversely, extreme neglect, can lay the groundwork for narcissistic tendencies.

Identifying the spectrum: Narcissism exists on a spectrum, from healthy self-esteem on one end to pathological narcissism, or NPD, on the other. It's critical to recognize that possessing confidence or taking pride in one's achievements doesn't necessarily make someone a narcissist. Pathological narcissism involves a pervasive pattern of grandiosity, a constant need for admiration, and a lack of empathy for others. Understanding this spectrum is crucial for recognizing when narcissistic traits veer into harmful territory, especially in the context of co-parenting.

The brain of a narcissist: Scientific studies have illuminated some of the neurological underpinnings of NPD, revealing differences in the cerebral cortex of individuals with narcissism. The cerebral cortex is involved in various higher-order functions, including empathy, emotional regulation, and judgment. In individuals with narcissism, areas of the cerebral cortex related to empathy and compassion may show reduced gray matter volume. This neurological basis helps explain the profound lack of empathy often observed in those with NPD, which manifests as an inability to recognize or respond to the emotional needs and boundaries of co-parents and children.

Impact of upbringing: The environment in which a person is raised can significantly influence the development of narcissistic traits. Being raised by narcissistic parents can set a precedent for narcissism, as children may model the behaviors and attitudes they observe. Similarly, growing up in an environment that excessively emphasizes achievement, appearance, or status can foster a superficial sense of self-worth which is tied to external validation rather than intrinsic values. These conditions create a fertile ground for the development of narcissistic behaviors, which can later complicate co-parenting dynamics.

While dissecting the psychology behind narcissism, it becomes evident that this condition is far from a black-and-white issue. The interplay of genetics and environmental factors, the existence of a narcissism spectrum, the neurological aspects, and the impact of upbringing all contribute to the complexity of narcissism. This understanding is not only crucial for those navigating co-parenting with a narcissist, but also for society's broader approach to recognizing and addressing narcissistic behaviors.

1.2 RECOGNIZING NARCISSISTIC BEHAVIOR IN YOUR EX

Navigating the waters of co-parenting requires a map that not only guides you through the logistics, but also helps you to understand the person you're dealing with, especially if they display narcissistic traits. Recognizing these behaviors is the first step to formulating a strategy that protects you and your children from potential emotional harm.

Spotting the Signs

Identifying narcissistic behaviors involves more than just observing a self-centered attitude. It's about noticing patterns of behavior that consistently puts their needs and desires above everyone else's, often at the expense of those around them. Key behaviors include:

- A relentless quest for admiration: Your ex might constantly seek validation and praise, not just from you but from everyone in their sphere, including your children. This behavior often involves boasting about achievements, exaggerating their importance in various scenarios, and fishing for compliments.
- Lack of empathy: This trait can be particularly damaging in the context of co-parenting. It manifests in an inability to consider or value the feelings and needs of others, including their own children. If your ex often dismisses or invalidates your children's emotions, it could be a sign of narcissistic behavior.
- Exploitation of relationships: Narcissists view relationships as tools to serve their own selves. This might mean manipulating you or the children to achieve

what they want, without regard for how it affects anyone else.

Many narcissists value friendships and relationships based on their utility - if they deem a connection to be beneficial to them in some way they will continue to invest in it, but the moment that the other person is no longer serving a purpose to them they are likely to walk away. For instance, in recent years I have discovered that a previous close friend of mine was a narcissist from analyzing their views and behavior. This friend, let's call him Bob, had a childhood best friend who did not have much confidence. Bob's best friend would follow him around, adhere to Bob's wishes, and be the subject of Bob's jokes and remarks which were often negative. However, this best friend eventually grew in confidence and came out of his shell thanks to new friendships, and Bob no longer had dominance/control over him. At this point Bob cut his best friend out of his life entirely despite their friendship spanning 12 years. Rather than valuing his best friend for who he is as a person, Bob valued him based on the extent to which he was useful in Bob's life, and the moment Bob could no longer use him, he dropped him like a discarded toy.

The Charm Offensive

At the beginning of relationships, and even in interactions following a separation, narcissists can employ their considerable charm and charisma to manipulate those around them. This "charm offensive" can be disarming—your ex might suddenly seem more cooperative or understanding, only to revert to manipulative behaviors once they've achieved their desired outcome. This tactic is not about genuine connection or compromise, but about controlling the narrative and the people within it to meet their needs.

Gaslighting and Reality Distortion

One of the most insidious tactics used by narcissists is gaslighting. This psychological manipulation aims to make you question your own memory, perception, or sanity. Examples include denying they said something which you clearly remember them saying, questioning your reactions to their inappropriate behavior, or painting you as the problematic one in front of your children or others. This tactic can leave you feeling confused, anxious, and doubting your own experiences.

Reaction to Criticism

Handling criticism is not a narcissist's strong suit. Their reaction to perceived slights or critiques, no matter how constructive, can range from cold withdrawal to outright aggression. This response stems from their fragile ego, which, despite their outward appearance of confidence, cannot tolerate the idea of imperfection or blame. Bob, the narcissist who I previously mentioned, considered himself to be an expert in our AP history class. However, when he was given helpful criticism on an essay he wrote, he angrily stormed out of class and didn't return. Similarly, in co-parenting scenarios, this behavior might manifest as explosive reactions to simple requests for cooperation or attempts to discuss parenting strategies.

Understanding these behaviors and their underlying motivations provides a crucial foundation for navigating co-parenting with a narcissistic ex. It arms you with the knowledge to anticipate potential issues and strategize your responses, ensuring that you and your children are shielded from the more harmful effects of these narcissistic tendencies.

1.3 THE IMPACT OF NARCISSISM ON RELATIONSHIPS

The ripple effects of narcissism on relationships stretch far beyond the immediate conflicts and misunderstandings. When one partner consistently prioritizes their needs and disregards others', it creates an environment ripe for emotional turmoil. The disregarded partner, and children, in this dynamic often bear invisible wounds, the depth and breadth of which can be difficult to measure, but impossible to ignore.

The Emotional Toll

Living with, or being closely connected to, a narcissist drains you emotionally. It's akin to being in a perpetual state of siege where your feelings are dismissed, your reality is questioned, and your self-esteem is systematically dismantled. The initial charm fades quickly, leaving behind a cycle of devaluation that can make you question your worth and sanity. Imagine constantly walking on eggshells, afraid that any action or word might trigger an outburst or cold withdrawal. This atmosphere breeds isolation, as friends and family may not understand the situation or why you can't just leave. Anxiety becomes a constant companion, and depression isn't far behind, as the joy in life dims under the shadow of a narcissistic partner's behavior.

Power Dynamics

Narcissists are masters of manipulation and are adept at creating and exploiting imbalances in relationships. This manipulation isn't always overt - it can be as subtle as shifting blame for their actions onto you, making you feel responsible for their happiness. They rely on tactics like gaslighting to erode your confidence in your perceptions and decisions, making you increasingly dependent on their version of reality. This dependency isn't created by accident, but by design, to ensure that you are too unsure of yourself to challenge their authority or the status quo. It's a calculated move to maintain control and keep you in a subordinate role, where your needs and wants are secondary, if considered at all.

The Cycle of Abuse

The relationship cycle with a narcissist can be broken down into three distinct phases: idealization, devaluation, and discarding. During the idealization phase, the narcissist showers you with affection and attention, making you feel like the most important person in the world. This phase is intoxicating but fleeting, as it's not rooted in genuine connection or respect. It's a means to an end, setting the stage for the devaluation phase, where that same affection turns to criticism, indifference, and often cruelty. The shift can be bewildering, leaving you desperate to regain the affection once freely given, often at the cost of your self-respect and dignity. Finally, the discarding phase occurs when the narcissist decides you no longer serve their needs, leaving you feeling abandoned and worthless. This cycle can repeat multiple times, each iteration chipping away at your self-esteem and sense of self-worth.

Long-term Effects

The scars left by a relationship with a narcissist can be deep and long-lasting. These scars aren't just emotional; they can manifest physically as well, in the form of stress-related illnesses or conditions exacerbated by constant anxiety and tension. The psychological impact, however, is often more difficult to recover from. Survivors of narcissistic relationships may struggle with trust issues, often fearing to open up or connect with others because of the fear of being manipulated or hurt again. They might also battle with codependency, having been conditioned to put others' needs before their own to avoid conflict. These long-term effects can ripple out, affecting future relationships and even how survivors parent their children, perpetuating a cycle of emotional dysfunction.

Living in the shadow of a narcissist, whether as a partner or co-parent, can take a heavy toll. The emotional, psychological, and sometimes physical consequences of such relationships necessitate not just awareness, but proactive measures to heal and rebuild a sense of self outside the influence of the narcissist's manipulative behaviors. Recognizing the impact of their behavior is the first step towards breaking free from the cycle of abuse and reclaiming your life and well-being.

1.4 NARCISSISTIC TACTICS AND HOW THEY MANIPULATE

Narcissists have a toolbox of manipulative tactics they employ to maintain control over their relationships. Understanding these tactics is crucial for anyone co-parenting with a narcissistic ex. It not only helps in recognizing when you're being manipulated, but also in developing strategies to counteract these behaviors.

Projection and Blame-Shifting

Narcissists often avoid taking responsibility for their actions by projecting their own undesirable traits onto others. This projection can be confusing and hurtful, as it attributes faults to you that are actually characteristics of the narcissist. For example, if they are being deceitful, they might accuse you of lying. Blame-shifting accompanies projection, where they manipulate situations to pin their mistakes and faults onto you. This tactic serves a dual purpose: it allows them to remain faultless in their eyes, while making you feel guilty and question your own actions.

Triangulation

Triangulation involves the use of a third party to manipulate a situation. Narcissists use triangulation to create competition, confusion, and conflicts among those around them, often between you and another person they bring into the dynamic. This could manifest in co-parenting scenarios where the narcissist might praise the parenting style of a friend or family member in comparison to yours, not to genuinely uplift that person, but to create insecurity and rivalry. The aim is to weaken your self-esteem and to pit individuals against each other, ensuring the narcissist remains in control and at the center of attention. A fantastic example of triangulation in action can be seen in series 9 of the sitcom *How I Met Your Mother* during episode 13 titled 'Bass Player Wanted'. During this episode a narcissist uses their charm to flatter and gain the trust of two people before putting them against each other.

Love Bombing and Devaluation

The cycle of love bombing and devaluation is a whirlwind of extreme highs and lows, designed to hook you emotionally and keep you off-balance. Love bombing is an overwhelming display of affection, attention, and admiration that occurs early in the relationship or at strategic points. It feels intoxicating, as the narcissist seems to put you on a pedestal, making you feel like the most important person in their world. However, this phase is short-lived and abruptly shifts to devaluation, where the same intensity is applied to criticizing, demeaning, and devaluing you. This sudden shift from being adored to devalued is disorienting and painful, making it difficult to leave the relationship because of the stark contrast to the affection once shown. In co-parenting, this might play out in how they treat you in front of the children, swinging from cooperative and overly friendly to dismissive and critical, leaving you, and potentially the children, confused about which version to expect.

Fear, Obligation, and Guilt (FOG)

FOG is a manipulation tactic involving fear, obligation, and guilt to control someone's actions and feelings. Narcissists adeptly use FOG as a way to keep their victims close and compliant.

- **Fear:** Narcissists instill fear of the consequences of not adhering to their wishes or demands. This might involve threats about taking you to court for every disagreement in co-parenting, or implications that you're unfit to parent, creating anxiety about potential loss or conflict. An example of fear being used to a narcissist's advantage involves a friend of mine who co-parents with a narcissistic ex. After several years, my friend moved on and entered a new relationship. When his ex, the mother of their three children, found out about the new partner from their son, she refused to let my friend see their daughter unless he ended the relationship. Faced with this ultimatum, my friend reluctantly agreed and did not see his daughter for a few weeks while trying to figure out his next steps. However, his narcissistic ex eventually grew tired of caring for their toddler full-time and allowed him to see his daughter again, despite his ongoing relationship. This situation clearly illustrates how narcissists use fear to control and manipulate others, dictating decisions based on their own desires and convenience.

- **Obligation:** They create a sense of obligation by recalling past instances where they were supportive or generous, often exaggerating these accounts, to make you feel indebted to them. This perceived obligation makes it difficult to say no or set boundaries, as you're reminded of what they've supposedly done for you.
- **Guilt:** Guilt is used to make you feel responsible for the narcissist's happiness and well-being, often suggesting that any failure on your part to comply with their needs or desires is selfish or harmful. In co-parenting, this could mean being guilted into changing agreed-upon plans or conceding to their demands for the sake of the children.

Recognizing these tactics is the first step in disengaging from the narcissist's manipulative grip. It allows you to view their actions through a lens of understanding and strategy, rather than getting caught up in the emotional turmoil they create. While it is certainly challenging, especially in the intricate dance of co-parenting, understanding these tactics empowers you to create boundaries, communicate effectively, and protect both your and your children's emotional well-being.

1.5 THE DIFFERENCE BETWEEN OVERT AND COVERT NARCISSISM

When delving into the complexities of narcissism, it's crucial to understand the distinction between its two main presentations: overt and covert narcissism. This differentiation not only aids in recognizing the type of narcissism you might be dealing with in a co-parent, but also informs the strategies you'll need to protect yourself and your children from their manipulative tactics.

Defining Overt Narcissism

Overt narcissism is the form most are familiar with. It's characterized by blatant self-centeredness, a palpable need for admiration, and a sense of entitlement that knows no bounds. Individuals with overt narcissistic traits are often the life of the party, exuding confidence and charm that can initially be quite magnetic. However, this facade belies a deeper need for constant validation and an inability to empathize with others. In co-parenting scenarios, an overt narcissist might openly demean your parenting skills in front of others or demand unreasonable changes to agreed-upon schedules, showcasing their dominance and disregard for your input.

Identifying Covert Narcissism

Covert narcissism, on the other hand, is more insidious and can be harder to detect. Those with covert traits display narcissism through defensiveness, sensitivity to criticism, and feelings of inadequacy that they mask with humility or self-deprecation. Unlike their overt counterparts, covert narcissists might not openly seek the spotlight but feel equally entitled to admiration and special treatment. This form of narcissism in a co-parent could manifest as playing the victim in every situation, subtly undermining your decisions regarding the children, or passive-aggressively resisting co-parenting agreements.

Impact on Relationships

Both forms of narcissism wreak havoc on relationships, albeit in different ways. Overt narcissists' blatant disregard for others can lead to overt conflicts, making co-parenting a battlefield where every interaction feels like a fight for respect and autonomy. The damage here is often visible, with clear instances of disrespect and manipulation.

Conversely, covert narcissists damage relationships through manipulation that's harder to pinpoint. Their passive-aggressive behavior and tendency to play the victim can sow seeds of doubt, guilt, and confusion, making you question your perceptions and decisions. This subtlety can make the manipulation by a covert narcissist more difficult to confront and resolve, as it's less visible and often couched in plausible deniability.

Strategies for Dealing With Narcissists

Understanding the type of narcissism you're dealing with in a co-parent allows you to tailor your approach to protect yourself and your children effectively. Here are some strategies for dealing with both overt and covert narcissists:

- **For Overt Narcissists:**
  - Maintain firm boundaries: Be clear and consistent about your boundaries. Overt narcissists will test these limits, so it's important to reinforce them consistently.
  - Document everything: Keep records of all communications and decisions. Their need for admiration and dominance may lead them to deny previous agreements or conversations.
  - Seek legal advice when necessary: Don't hesitate to consult a legal professional if the narcissist's behavior crosses legal boundaries, especially concerning your children's welfare.
- **For Covert Narcissists:**
  - Recognize manipulation tactics: Learn to identify passive-aggressive behaviors and victim-playing as forms of manipulation. Acknowledging these tactics can help you in not taking them personally and thus responding more objectively.
  - Communicate in writing: This minimizes the chances of misinterpretation and manipulation. Written communication provides a record that can clarify misunderstandings or deliberate distortions of your words.
  - Use neutral language: Avoid emotionally charged language or insults that could give the narcissist ammunition to play the victim or accuse you of being unreasonable.

In both cases, prioritizing your and your children's emotional well-being is key. This might mean limiting direct communication with the narcissistic co-parent to only essential topics regarding the children. In addition it would also be beneficial to seek support from professionals, such as therapists familiar with narcissistic behaviors, to navigate the complex emotional landscape of co-parenting under these circumstances.

Understanding the nuances between overt and covert narcissism illuminates the specific challenges each presents in co-parenting dynamics. Armed with this knowledge, you can develop tailored strategies to mitigate their impact, ensuring a healthier and more stable environment for your children.

2

MASTERING COMMUNICATION
WITHOUT CONFLICT

In a world where words can either be bridges or barriers, co-parenting with a narcissistic ex often feels like walking through a minefield blindfolded. Every conversation holds the potential for conflict, misunderstanding, or manipulation. Maneuvering through this landscape demands not just caution, but a strategic approach to communication that minimizes harm while protecting your integrity and the well-being of your children.

Maintaining Consistency for Children

- **Create routines:** Establish routines for your children that remain consistent regardless of which parent they are with. This could include regular meal times, bedtimes, and activities. Routines offer children a sense of security amidst the unpredictable. For instance, if your child attends a swimming club on Tuesday nights, ensure that this arrangement is adhered to consistently so that the child is confident in their weekly routine.
- **Unified parenting front:** As much as possible, try to agree on basic parenting approaches and rules with your narcissistic ex. This might involve using mediation or a neutral third party to facilitate these discussions. It's about making sure your kids see that parental guidance is consistent, even if parental unity isn't perfect.

Navigating the Power Struggles

Power struggles are to be expected when co-parenting with a narcissist, but engaging in them can exacerbate the chaos, which in turn affects your well-being and that of your children. Consider these strategies to navigate these struggles:

- **Pick your battles:** Not every disagreement needs to escalate into a conflict. Determine which issues genuinely

warrant a stand and which ones can be let go for the sake of peace.
- **Stay focused on the children's needs:** In all interactions and decisions, keep the focus on what is best for the children. This helps in steering conversations away from personal conflicts and towards cooperative parenting.

Amidst this precarious balancing act, there lies a strategy as simple as it is effective: becoming the gray rock. This method isn't about winning or losing, but about safeguarding your peace and ensuring that the well-being of your children remains the focal point of every interaction.

2.1 THE ART OF GRAY ROCK: COMMUNICATING WITHOUT CONFLICT

Emotional Neutrality

The core of the gray rock method lies in presenting yourself as uninteresting as a rock. Think about it: a gray rock doesn't evoke strong emotions - it doesn't react, retaliate, or engage. By adopting a demeanor that is as unresponsive as possible to the narcissist's attempts to provoke you, you effectively remove the fuel they thrive on—emotional reaction. This doesn't mean becoming emotionless, but rather choosing not to display your emotions during interactions with the narcissistic ex.

- **When:** Especially useful in face-to-face encounters or during phone calls - any interaction with the potential to escalate.
- **How:** Keep your responses as brief and neutral as possible; make sure they are devoid of any emotional content and

are purely factual. If they try to bait you with a snide remark about your parenting, a simple "I see" or "Okay" will suffice, this will then allow you to redirect the conversation to the matter at hand.
- **Why:** It discourages further attempts at provocation, as the narcissist learns that their tactics no longer elicit a response.

Maintaining Composure

Keeping your cool when faced with aggression or manipulation is no small feat. It's like trying to stay calm when someone cuts you off in traffic. Your initial reaction might be to honk your horn and retaliate, but what does that achieve? Instead, taking a deep breath and focusing on your destination is more productive. The same goes for dealing with a narcissistic ex.

- **Techniques:** Practice deep breathing exercises or have a 'calm down' playlist on your phone. Before responding to a provocation, take a moment to breathe or listen to a calming tune.
- **Why:** This helps reset your emotional state, allowing you to respond from a place of calm rather than react out of anger.

Predicting Triggers

Knowing what sets off the narcissist—and you—is like having a weather forecast for your interactions. Just as you'd carry an umbrella if rain is predicted, you can prepare yourself for potential triggers.

- **Identify:** Reflect on past interactions. Which topics or comments have sparked conflict?
- **Prepare:** Have neutral responses ready for these triggers. Think of them as your conversational umbrella, keeping you dry from the storm of conflict.
- **Avoid:** If possible, steer clear of these topics altogether. If they can't be avoided, stick to factual, unemotional responses.

Choosing Your Battles

Recognizing the difference between issues that merit confrontation and those that are traps for manipulation is akin to developing a sixth sense. It's about distinguishing between what's critical for your children's welfare and what's a provocation designed to entangle you in unnecessary conflict. This discernment is crucial—it conserves your energy for matters of genuine importance and deprives the narcissist of the conflict they seek to create. For instance, disagreeing on minor changes in pickup times might not be as consequential as disputes over major health decisions. Identifying this distinction helps in focusing your efforts where they're most needed, ensuring that your children's needs remain paramount.

Consistency is Key

For the gray rock method to be effective, consistency is non-negotiable. An occasional slip into emotional reaction can reset the cycle, encouraging the narcissist to continue their attempts to manipulate. Consistency signals that the change in your response pattern is permanent, not a temporary phase.

- **Who:** This applies to you in all of your interactions related to co-parenting.
- **What:** Maintain the same level of emotional neutrality, regardless of the provocation.
- **Where:** This approach should be used in all settings, whether in public, at home, or during mediation sessions.

Remember, the goal isn't to change the narcissist's behavior—that's out of your control—but to protect your peace and stability.

- **Set reminders:** It can be helpful to set periodic reminders on your phone or write notes to yourself about staying the course, especially before anticipated interactions with your ex.
- **Reflect:** Regularly take time to reflect on how this method has impacted your co-parenting dynamic. Adjust your approach as needed, but always within the framework of minimizing conflict.

Protecting Your Energy

View the gray rock method as a form of self-preservation. Engaging in emotional battles with a narcissist is draining, and leaves you with less energy for yourself and, importantly, your children. By refusing to engage, you conserve your emotional and mental energy.

- **Real-life example:** Think of a time when an argument with the narcissist left you feeling exhausted and upset for days. Now imagine that instead, you had remained calm and unaffected during the interaction, thus preserving your peace and energy.

For instance, I recall a time when I had a heated argument with my narcissistic ex about a simple scheduling change for our child's activities. What should have been a straightforward conversation quickly escalated, with accusations being thrown my way, leaving me emotionally drained and upset for days. I couldn't stop replaying the argument, second-guessing myself, and feeling overwhelmed by the conflict.

Now imagine that instead, I had remained calm and unaffected, that I had used a tool like a co-parenting app to communicate, kept my boundaries intact, and refused to engage with their emotional manipulation. By remaining composed, I would have preserved my peace and energy, and left the interaction with a clear mind while avoiding the emotional toll that these conflicts so often take.

Impact on Children

Children are astute observers and often pick up on and mimic the communication styles of their parents. Demonstrating a model of calm and controlled communication teaches them valuable lessons about handling conflict and emotional regulation.

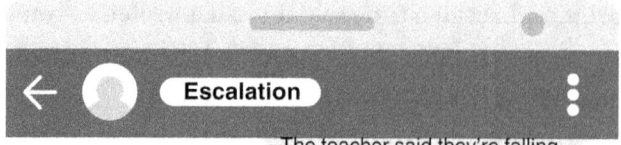

> The teacher said they're falling behind. This is on you.

Of course you'd blame me!

> You're doing the homework routine all wrong. No wonder the kids are behind in school. They need structure, which you clearly don't give them.

That's not true! The routine I set up works.

> Your 'routine' is a joke. If I were in charge, they'd be top of their class

I work hard! You're just looking for a reason to criticize.

> You never listen. You're holding them back with your laziness.

 I'm doing all the work while you do nothing!

MASTERING COMMUNICATION WITHOUT CONFLICT | 35

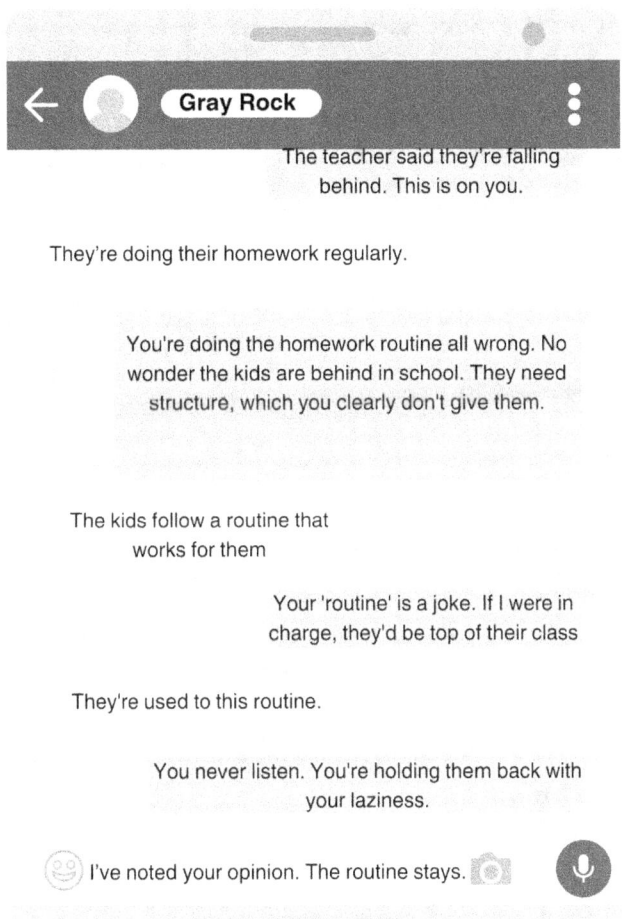

Cycle of Conflict Escalation vs. the Cycle of De-escalation Using the Gray Rock Method

It may be helpful to use the following journaling prompts to reflect on your past experiences with the gray rock method, explore situations where it may have been helpful, and plan how to effectively use this technique in future interactions. Take your time to think deeply and honestly about each question, and consider writing down any insights or patterns that emerge.

Reflecting on Past Successes:

1. **Describe a time when you successfully used the gray rock method in a conversation or situation with your ex.**
    - What triggered your decision to use this method?_____
    _____
    _____

    - How did you feel while using it?_____
    _____
    _____

    - What was the outcome, both immediately and in the long term?_____
    _____
    _____

2. **How did your ex react when you employed the gray rock technique?**
    - Did their behavior change?_____
    _____
    _____

    - Did it affect your relationship or communication style moving forward?_____
    _____
    _____

3. **What strategies helped you stay calm and neutral during the interaction?**
    - Did you use any specific techniques, such as deep breathing or reminding yourself of your goals?_____
    _____
    _____

Reflecting on Missed Opportunities:

1. **Think of a time when you wish you had used the gray rock method but didn't.**
    - What emotions or thoughts prevented you from using it?_____
    _____
    _____
    - How did the situation escalate as a result?_____
    _____
    _____
    - What might have happened if you had chosen to be more neutral?_____
    _____
    _____

2. **Looking back, what could you have done differently in that moment?**
    - How might using the gray rock method have altered the dynamic?_____
    _____
    _____
    - Would it have provided more emotional distance or control?_____
    _____
    _____

Planning for Future Situations:

1. **Identify potential triggers in your co-parenting relationship that could lead to conflict.**
    - How can you anticipate using the gray rock method in these situations? _____
    _____
    _____

    - What might you say or do to remain emotionally neutral? _____
    _____
    _____

2. **Describe a scenario where you believe employing the gray rock method would be beneficial.**
    - How do you plan to respond with minimal emotion and engagement? _____
    _____
    _____

    - What is your desired outcome in this scenario? _____
    _____
    _____

3. **How can you prepare yourself mentally and emotionally to use the gray rock method when needed?**
    - Are there specific phrases or actions you can rehearse to stay on track? _____
    _____
    _____

Self-Reflection:

1. **What emotional benefits have you experienced from using the gray rock method?**
    - How has it contributed to your overall well-being?_____
    _____
    _____

    - Has it shifted the power dynamic in your co-parenting relationship?_____
    _____
    _____

2. **What advice would you give to someone who is struggling to implement the gray rock technique?**
    - What has been the most challenging aspect for you, and how have you overcome it?_____
    _____
    _____

By adopting the gray rock method, you're not just avoiding unnecessary conflict; you're also setting a powerful example to your children of how to manage difficult situations with grace and emotional intelligence. It's about making a conscious choice to prioritize your well-being and that of your children over the drama and negativity that often accompanies interactions with a narcissistic ex.

2.2 SETTING THE STAGE: STRUCTURED COMMUNICATION PLATFORMS

In the realm of co-parenting, particularly with a narcissistic ex-partner, the medium of communication can significantly influence the outcome of an interaction. The choice of *how* we exchange information can either fuel the fire of conflict or act as a dampener, by reducing the oxygen that feeds the flames of discord. This is where specialized co-parenting platforms come into play, as they offer a structured environment designed to keep communication focused, documented, and less personal. When direct communication becomes too charged, using neutral third parties or communication apps specifically designed for co-parenting, such as OurFamilyWizard, TalkingParents, or 2Houses, can help mitigate conflicts by providing structured communication and clear documentation.

Choosing the Right Tools

Selecting an appropriate communication platform is akin to picking the right tool for a job as it can make all the difference in efficiency and effectiveness. Co-parenting platforms are built with the unique challenges of shared parenting in mind and incorporate features that promote organization and cooperation while minimizing conflict. When evaluating these tools, consider the following:

- **Ease of Use:** The platform should be user-friendly for both parents, encouraging regular use without a steep learning curve.
- **Features:** Look for features that address your specific needs, such as shared calendars, expense tracking, and secure messaging.
- **Privacy and Security:** Ensure the platform has robust security measures to protect your personal information and communication.
- **Recommendations:** Seek recommendations from other co-parents or professionals, like family therapists and

lawyers, who might have insights into the most effective tools.

Finding a platform that fits seamlessly into your co-parenting routine can transform how you and your ex-partner communicate, and lay the groundwork for more constructive interactions.

Boundaries in Communication

Structured communication platforms inherently reinforce boundaries. By design, they keep exchanges focused on the children and co-parenting logistics, discouraging any venture into personal territory that can lead to conflict. For instance:

- **Designated Topics:** Many platforms allow for conversations to be categorized, ensuring that discussions remain on topic, whether about scheduling, health concerns, or educational matters.
- **Scheduled Updates:** Some tools enable parents to schedule updates, which can help in maintaining regular communication without the need for constant back-and-forth messaging.

These platforms act as a buffer by maintaining a professional-like distance between co-parents, which is crucial when dealing with a narcissistic ex-partner prone to using communication as a battleground.

Neutral Language

In every message or conversation with a narcissistic ex, your choice of words matters profoundly. Using neutral language—free of emotional charge, accusation, or ambiguity—can significantly reduce the narcissist's ammunition for creating conflict. This approach is about sticking to facts and specifics, and avoiding any language that could be interpreted as provocative or judgmental. For example, instead of saying, "You always pick the kids up late," opt for, "Let's confirm the pickup time to ensure consistency for the kids." This method not only helps in defusing potential conflicts, but also models constructive communication for your children, teaching them valuable skills in expressing their needs and resolving disagreements.

Reducing Direct Contact

Direct interactions with a narcissistic ex-partner can be emotionally draining and are often fraught with the potential for conflict. Structured communication platforms offer an alternative, reducing the need for face-to-face or telephonic conversations, which are more likely to go off the rails. This reduction in direct contact has several benefits:

- **Minimizes Emotional Stress:** Less direct contact means fewer opportunities for the narcissist to engage in emotional manipulation or provocation.
- **Focuses on Parenting:** With communication limited to the platform, discussions are more likely to stay on topic and centered around co-parenting rather than personal grievances.
- **Creates a Safe Space:** For those who have experienced emotional abuse, minimizing direct contact can feel like a reprieve, creating a safer space to focus on healing and moving forward.

By carefully selecting a structured communication platform and utilizing its features to enforce boundaries, document interactions, and minimize direct contact, co-parents can create a more manageable and less contentious environment. This approach not only benefits the parents but also, and most importantly, creates a more stable and peaceful backdrop for the children involved.

2.3 DOCUMENTING EVERYTHING: THE IMPORTANCE OF WRITTEN RECORDS

In the delicate balance of co-parenting with a narcissistic ex, the pen—or in today's digital age, the keyboard—holds power unparalleled by any spoken word. The act of documenting every interaction, decision, and agreement isn't merely about keeping records; it's a strategic move that shields you from the whirlwinds of manipulation and ensures that the focus remains on what matters most: the well-being of your children. One of the most valuable aspects of using a structured communication platform is the automatic documentation it provides. Every message sent, every agreement made, and every schedule change requested is logged and easily accessible.

Legal Protection

The significance of documentation extends far beyond personal preference into the realm of legal necessity. In disputes or when custody arrangements are under scrutiny, having a detailed account of interactions, agreements, and incidents can make a substantial difference. It's not uncommon for narcissistic ex-partners to challenge previously made decisions or to deny statements they made in the past. Here, your documentation becomes your steadfast ally, offering clear, incontrovertible evidence that can support your position and help uphold the integrity of custody arrangements and agreements.

- In instances where verbal agreements about visitation or parenting responsibilities are contested, written records can provide clarity and proof of consensus.
- During legal proceedings, emails, text messages, and official documents serve as evidence of each parent's involvement, commitment, and adherence to stipulated guidelines.

Memory Aid

One of the more insidious tactics employed by narcissistic individuals is gaslighting—making you question your memory, perception, and sanity. This psychological manipulation can leave you doubting your experiences and decisions. Here, your meticulously kept records serve as an anchor to reality. They offer a reliable account of conversations and events, allowing you to trust your recollections and stand firm in your knowledge of the truth.

- Maintaining a log or journal where you note down key conversations, decisions, and events soon after they occur ensures you have an accurate record of events.
- Utilizing emails and text messages for important communications, rather than face-to-face interaction, provides a date-stamped record that can be referenced when memory alone might falter.

Clarity and Accountability

Clarity in co-parenting arrangements is not just beneficial, it's essential. Written records ensure that agreements, from broad parenting plans, to minute details like who buys the winter coats this year, are clear, explicit, and traceable. This level of detail not only minimizes confusion but also fosters accountability. When expectations are documented, it's much harder for a narcissistic ex to feign ignorance or to shift goalposts. Each parent knows precisely what's expected of them, and there's a tangible reference point for discussions if disagreements arise.

- For every agreement reached, whether through informal negotiation or formal mediation, follow up with a written summary that outlines the key points and expectations.
- Use shared digital calendars for scheduling, ensuring that both parents have access to and can agree on the children's activities, appointments, and visitations. A good app for this would be Cozi, which offers a free version and includes features like shared calendars, reminders, and to-do lists to keep both parents organized and informed. You can find it by scanning this code:

Choosing What to Document

While the impulse might be to document every interaction for the sake of thoroughness, focusing on key communications that have legal, financial, or health-related implications is most effective. This selective approach not only saves time but also ensures your energy is concentrated on matters of significance.

- **Legal Implications:** Document all interactions that could have legal ramifications, including those related to custody, visitation rights, and any instances where the well-being of the child is at stake.
- **Financial Transactions:** Keep records of all financial transactions related to child support, shared expenses, and any agreed-upon contributions to savings accounts for the children's future needs.
- **Health-Related Issues:** Document discussions and decisions regarding the children's health, including medical appointments, treatments, and health emergencies. This ensures that both parents are informed and involved in the health and well-being of their children.

The process of documenting every pertinent aspect of co-parenting with a narcissistic ex might seem daunting, yet it's a practice imbued with wisdom and foresight. Documentation is about more than creating a paper trail - it establishes a foundation of truth and accountability to guard yourself against manipulation, foster clear communication, and uphold the sanctity of agreements made in the best interest of the children. In the labyrinth of co-parenting with a narcissist, your documented records act as the thread that will guide you through, ensuring that amidst the chaos, the focus remains steadfastly on nurturing and protecting your children.

2.4 DECIPHERING MANIPULATIVE MESSAGES: READING BETWEEN THE LINES

In the digital age, the written word carries immense power, particularly in the context of co-parenting with someone displaying narcissistic tendencies. Their messages can sometimes feel like a trap which is littered with hidden motives and manipulative tactics. Recognizing these tactics is the first step to maintaining your emotional equilibrium and ensuring your responses serve your best interests and those of your children.

Recognizing Manipulation

Narcissists have a knack for embedding manipulation within their communication. Their messages may contain guilt trips, subtle threats, or attempts to sow doubt about your perceptions and decisions. Identifying these manipulative strategies involves paying close attention to:

- **Inconsistencies:** Messages that contradict previous statements or known facts can be attempts to confuse and undermine your confidence.
- **Emotional triggers:** Phrases or words chosen to elicit an emotional response, like guilt or anger, are often used to manipulate you into compliance or to destabilize your decision-making.
- **Veiled threats:** Sometimes, a message may include indirect threats, such as suggesting potential legal action or implying negative consequences regarding your parenting time, aimed at intimidation.
- **False accusations:** Accusing you of behaviors or attitudes you don't exhibit can be a tactic to put you on the defensive and shift the focus away from legitimate concerns you've raised.

By staying vigilant and critically assessing the content and tone of the messages you receive, you can start to discern patterns of manipulation and arm yourself with the insight needed to navigate these communications strategically.

Staying Objective

Maintaining objectivity in the face of manipulative messages is akin to navigating through a storm without losing your direction. It requires a steadfast commitment to forbid your emotions from dictating your responses. Strategies to help include:

- **Pausing before responding:** Giving yourself time to process the message and detach from any immediate emotional reactions allows you to formulate a more measured and effective response.
- **Focusing on facts:** Center your responses (if necessary) on factual information relevant to the co-parenting arrangement, thus enabling you to sidestep the emotional bait.
- **Seeking third-party perspectives:** Sometimes, sharing the message with a trusted friend or advisor can help you see the manipulation more clearly and decide on an appropriate response.
- **Changing your viewpoint:** Imagine that your best friend is in your shoes and think about the advice you would give to them. Imagining the messages have been sent to someone who we care about can make it easier for us to see the sender's intentions more clearly.

These strategies act as anchors, keeping you grounded in rationality and preventing you from being swept away by the emotional currents of manipulative messages.

Response Strategies

Crafting responses to manipulative messages is a delicate balance between asserting your boundaries and avoiding escalation. The goal is not to "win" but to communicate effectively within the confines of necessary co-parenting interactions. Here are some guidelines for crafting your responses:

- **Keep it brief:** Lengthy explanations or justifications invite further manipulation. Stick to short, clear responses that address only the necessary points.
- **Avoid emotional language:** Even when provoked, resist the urge to respond in kind. Use neutral, polite language that keeps the conversation focused on co-parenting matters.
- **Reinforce boundaries:** If a message crosses a boundary, calmly restate that boundary and your expectations. For example, "As we agreed, all communication about schedule changes needs to be confirmed through the co-parenting app."

These response strategies not only help in managing the immediate situation, but also in gradually shifting the dynamics of your communication, making it clear that manipulative tactics will not yield the desired results.

Teaching Resilience

Our children are often silent witnesses to the dynamics of co-parenting and learn from our actions and responses. Utilizing experiences with manipulative messages as teaching moments can equip them with invaluable lessons in communication and resilience:

- **Modeling healthy communication:** Show your children how to communicate respectfully, even in difficult situations, with an emphasis on the importance of clear,

honest, and respectful dialogue.
- **Discussing boundary setting:** Use age-appropriate language to explain the concept of boundaries and why they're important in all relationships, not just with family members.
- **Encouraging emotional intelligence:** Teach your children to recognize their emotions and express them healthily and constructively. This will foster an environment where they feel safe to share their thoughts and feelings.

These lessons in resilience, grounded in the real-world context of navigating communication with a narcissistic ex, provide your children with a strong foundation for handling their own interpersonal relationships effectively and with integrity.

In the journey of co-parenting with a narcissistic ex, messages laden with manipulation can create significant stress and challenges. However, by learning to recognize these tactics, maintaining objectivity, crafting strategic responses, and using these experiences as teachable moments for your children, you build a fortress of resilience. This not only protects your peace, but also ensures that the co-parenting path, while complex, is navigated with wisdom, strength, and a focus on the well-being of the children at its heart.

2.5 THE POWER OF BREVITY: KEEPING COMMUNICATION SHORT AND SWEET

In the nuanced landscape of co-parenting with a narcissist, less is often more—especially when it comes to communication. Stripping down your interactions to the essentials not only diminishes the narcissist's playground for manipulation but also streamlines your exchanges, making them less taxing and more manageable. Here, we explore the art of brevity in communication, a skill that, when mastered, can transform your co-parenting experience.

Avoiding Unnecessary Details

Sharing too much information or delving into emotional explanations provides a narcissist with multiple avenues to critique, manipulate, or twist your words. By limiting the details you share, you reduce these opportunities and keep the focus squarely on the matter at hand—your children's welfare. This approach requires a mental shift towards viewing communication as a transaction rather than a dialogue, where the goal is to convey necessary information as efficiently as possible.

- **Practice:** Before sending a message or responding to one, take a moment to strip down your response to its most basic elements. Ask yourself, "What does the other parent really need to know?". Use the notes page on your phone, or a pen and paper, to write out your message first and make sure it communicates all of the necessary information without giving any ammunition to your narcissistic ex.

Clear and Concise Communication

Clarity and conciseness in your messages serve as the backbone of effective communication with a narcissistic ex. This means being direct and to the point, avoiding ambiguous language that could be misinterpreted or manipulated. It's about finding the shortest path to convey your message without sacrificing its integrity.

- **Techniques:** Use bullet points to break down information, making it easily digestible. Start with the most important point, followed by any necessary details, and make sure they are each succinctly stated.

Reducing Engagement

The more you engage, the more you invite further communication—and with a narcissist, this often means more conflict and manipulation. By keeping your messages brief, you naturally limit the scope of the conversation. It's a subtle way of setting boundaries, signaling that you're only available for essential co-parenting communication, not endless debates or emotional entanglements.

- **Implementation:** Set a personal rule for yourself, such as limiting your responses to no more than three sentences, or using only factual statements without personal commentary.

Modeling for Children

Children absorb not just the content of what we communicate, but *how* we communicate. Demonstrating brevity and clarity in your interactions teaches them valuable lessons in communication. They learn that it's possible to express needs, boundaries, and information in a way that's respectful yet firm. This skill is invaluable, and you will be equipping them with the tools to navigate their own relationships effectively.

- **Example:** When discussing co-parenting arrangements in front of your children, use clear and concise language. Show them that even complex situations can be discussed in a calm and straightforward manner.

The power of brevity in communicating with a narcissist cannot be overstated. It's a strategy that serves multiple purposes: it minimizes the narcissist's room for manipulation, streamlines your interactions to make them less emotionally draining, and sets a positive example of effective communication for your children. Moreover, this approach fosters an environment where conversations are less about the power struggle and more about the practical aspects of co-parenting.

As we conclude this exploration of communication strategies, remember that the goal is always to focus on what best serves you and your children's needs. The tactics discussed are not about disengagement from meaningful dialogue, but about protecting your peace and creating a co-parenting dynamic that prioritizes the well-being of your children above all. Moving forward, let's carry these lessons into every interaction, crafting a path that leads to a more harmonious and effective co-parenting relationship.

3

BOUNDARIES - THE BLUEPRINT FOR PEACE

When co-parenting with a narcissistic ex, boundaries are not just helpful, they are your armor. Boundaries safeguard your mental peace, protect your children from unnecessary stress, and delineate the lines your narcissistic co-parent should not cross. Picture this: You're planning a garden - not just any garden, but one that will flourish and bring joy for years to come. The first step? Laying out the boundaries. Without them, your flowers might get trampled, or weeds could invade. This garden is a lot like co-parenting with a narcissistic ex. Boundaries act as both the framework and the protective barrier, ensuring that growth can take place within a safe, defined space. It's not about building walls, but rather defining where your space begins and ends, allowing for healthy interactions and your personal well-being to thrive.

However, setting and maintaining these boundaries is easier said than done. It demands clarity, consistency, and a fair amount of courage. Let's explore how to effectively establish these necessary limits and ensure they are respected.

3.1 IDENTIFYING NON-NEGOTIABLE BOUNDARIES

Core Values and Safety

At the heart of boundary-setting is understanding what you stand for and what you absolutely cannot compromise on. It's like knowing that your garden needs sunlight as without it, nothing will grow. Core values might include respect, honesty, and safety. When these are threatened, it impacts not just you, but your children too. Think about behavior which crosses the line - is it verbal aggression? Undermining your parenting? Or exposing the kids to unhealthy situations? Identifying these non-negotiables is the first step in creating a boundary blueprint.

Specificity is Crucial

Clear boundaries specify the behaviors you will tolerate, how communication should occur, and the consequences of overstepping these limits. Setting boundaries is about explicitly stating what is acceptable and what isn't, both for your sanity and for the well-being of your children. Be explicit and specific; vague boundaries are easily ignored or manipulated. Define them clearly. For instance, instead of saying "I need space," specify "I will not answer calls or texts between 8 p.m. and 8 a.m. unless it's an emergency involving the children." Similarly, "be respectful" sounds good, but is too vague to enforce. Instead, be as specific as possible. If respect means not raising voices during exchanges, state it clearly. It's like telling someone not to just water the plants, but to give them exactly one inch of water weekly. This clarity removes ambiguity and sets clear expectations. Focus on actionable items; your boundaries should focus on actions and behaviors. For example, the message "All communication about the children must be done through [specific co-parenting app]" provides a clear, actionable guideline.

Flexibility in Non-Essentials

Not everything is a hill to die on. Some things require firm boundaries, but others might allow for flexibility. Maybe you're strict about bedtime on school nights but more lenient about weekend bedtimes. Recognizing where you can bend without breaking is key to maintaining balance and avoiding unnecessary conflict.

Communicating Boundaries Clearly

Once you've identified your boundaries, the next hurdle is communicating them in a straightforward and assertive manner which leaves no room for misunderstanding. It's not about throwing a rulebook at your ex, but having a clear, calm conversation about what these boundaries are and why they're important. Imagine you're explaining the rules of a board game to ensure everyone plays fairly - this is the same principle. This might mean writing them down and discussing them over a co-parenting app, during a mediation session, or simply wherever you can speak openly and without interruptions. Written communication can be beneficial here, as it will provide a clear record which can be referred back to if needed.

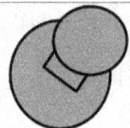

Check List...

- ☐ **Identify Your Non-Negotiables**
  What values and behaviors are essential? (e.g., respect, safety, clear communication)
- ☐ **Be Specific and Clear**
  Define acceptable and unacceptable behaviors clearly. Avoid vague terms.
- ☐ **Set Consequences for Boundary Violations**
  Decide the actions you will take if a boundary is crossed.
- ☐ **Communicate Boundaries Assertively**
  Share your boundaries in a calm, direct manner, either through conversation or writing.
- ☐ **Stick to Your Boundaries Consistently**
  Enforce the boundaries by following through on the consequences if they are violated.
- ☐ **Use Written Communication When Necessary**
  Utilize co-parenting apps, emails, or mediation to document boundaries when needed.
- ☐ **Allow Flexibility in Non-Essentials**
  Recognize which boundaries are firm and where you can be flexible (e.g., weekend vs. school night routines).

You can use this template to assert your boundaries calmly and confidently, ensuring both your mental well-being and your children's needs remain protected.

Boundary Communication Letter Template

Dear [Co-parent's Name],

I hope you're well. I want to take a moment to communicate some important boundaries that I believe will help us co-parent more effectively and ensure that the children's well-being remains our priority.

1. **Specific Boundary:** [Clearly state your boundary. For example: "I will not respond to calls or texts after 8 p.m. unless it's an emergency involving the children."]
   - **Reasoning:** [Explain why this boundary is important to you. For example: "Maintaining this boundary helps ensure that I can rest and recharge, which ultimately benefits the children and our co-parenting relationship."]
2. **Specific Boundary:** [Clearly state another boundary. For example: "All communication regarding the children should be conducted through the co-parenting app."]
   - **Reasoning:** [Explain why this boundary is important. For example: "Using the app helps keep communication clear and prevents any misunderstandings. It also provides a written record that we can both reference."]
3. **Specific Boundary:** [Clearly state another boundary. For example: "When discussing parenting decisions, I expect that we maintain respectful communication, meaning no raising voices or insults."]
   - **Reasoning:** [Explain why this boundary is necessary. For example: "It's important to me that our discussions remain calm and focused on the children's best interests, without any unnecessary conflict."]

I believe these boundaries will help create a healthier co-parenting dynamic for both of us and, most importantly, for the children. I would appreciate it if you could respect these boundaries moving forward.

If you have any concerns or need further clarification, I'm open to discussing them in a respectful manner.

Thank you for your understanding and cooperation.

Sincerely,
[Your Name]

In every instance, remember that the goal of setting boundaries isn't to control or punish the other parent, but to create a safe, predictable environment which enables your children to thrive. It's about laying down the garden paths that will lead you through co-parenting with a sense of direction and purpose.

3.2 IMPLEMENTING BOUNDARIES WITHOUT ESCALATION

When it comes to setting the stage for a non-confrontational co-parenting environment, the implementation of boundaries without causing further conflict can feel like walking a tightrope. It requires a blend of steadfastness and diplomacy, especially when managing the delicate dynamics with a narcissistic ex. Here's how to tread this path with care, ensuring that boundaries reinforce the structure needed for a harmonious co-parenting relationship while minimizing the risk of escalation.

Consistent Enforcement

One of the cornerstones of effective boundary management is the unwavering enforcement of established limits. It's about creating an environment where expectations are clear and predictable, much like setting a daily routine that brings a sense of security and stability. This approach doesn't just apply to the children - it extends to your interactions with your ex-partner as well. By consistently applying the same rules and responses to boundary violations, you signal that these aren't arbitrary lines drawn in the sand but non-negotiable standards for interaction. For instance, if you have stated that you will not engage in communication outside specific hours, stick to it, no matter the provocation. Use consequences wisely. If a boundary is crossed, follow through with the stated consequences. For example, if excessive calls continue, reiterate your boundary and then block their number during the hours you've specified as off-limits. Consistency here serves multiple purposes:

- It provides a clear framework within which both parents can operate, this reduces misunderstandings and misinterpretations.
- It sends a message to the narcissistic ex that these boundaries are firmly in place, reducing their attempts to test or cross these limits. The true test of a boundary is in its enforcement. Without follow-through, boundaries are merely suggestions. Narcissistic individuals may test these limits repeatedly, requiring you to be firm and consistent in your responses.

Seeking Support

Navigating co-parenting with a narcissistic ex is not a solo venture. Leaning on your support network and professionals who understand the dynamics at play can provide not just emotional comfort, but also practical strategies for enforcing boundaries. This support system could include:

- Friends and family members who offer a listening ear and practical help when needed, providing a respite from the stresses of co-parenting.
- Therapists or counselors who can offer guidance on handling interactions with your ex, reinforcing your resolve, and providing tools for managing difficult conversations.

- Legal professionals who can advise on the enforcement of boundaries through legal channels if necessary, ensuring you're aware of your rights and options.

This network acts as both a buffer and a resource, empowering you to enforce boundaries with the knowledge that you're not alone in this endeavor.

Protecting Personal Space

Creating and protecting personal space, both physically and emotionally, is essential when co-parenting with a narcissistic ex. This space is your sanctuary, a place where the turmoil of co-parenting negotiations cannot intrude. Strategies for maintaining this personal space include:

- Setting clear physical boundaries regarding your home and personal time, and ensuring that your ex understands and respects these limits.
- Engaging in activities that bolster your emotional well-being, from hobbies that bring you joy, to exercise that strengthens your body and mind, thus fortifying your emotional defenses.
- Limiting direct communication with your ex to necessary co-parenting discussions, and utilizing co-parenting apps or email for these exchanges so that you can maintain a degree of separation.
- Cultivating mindfulness or meditation practices that help center you, and keep the stresses of co-parenting from overwhelming your sense of peace and stability.

These practices are not just about creating barriers, but about nurturing a space where you can recharge and rejuvenate. This ensures that you have the resilience to manage co-parenting challenges effectively.

Implementing boundaries with a narcissistic ex relies on consistency, careful communication, support, and maintaining a personal sanctuary.. These elements work together to maintain a stable co-parenting environment, minimize conflict, and manufacture a setting where your children can thrive, free from the turbulence of parental discord.

3.3 WHEN BOUNDARIES ARE CROSSED: ENFORCEMENT STRATEGIES

Boundaries, in the realm of co-parenting with a narcissist, are akin to the rules of the road—they keep everyone moving in the right direction and ensure safety. However, when these boundaries are disregarded, it disrupts the flow, creating confusion and potential harm. The key to dealing with these transgressions lies in a well-thought-out strategy for enforcement, a plan that not only addresses the immediate breach but also reinforces the importance of these guidelines for future interactions.

Consequences and Follow-Through

The effectiveness of a boundary hinges on the consequences tied to it and the unwavering commitment to enforce them. When a boundary is crossed, it's crucial to act, not out of retaliation, but to underscore the significance of these established limits. Here's how:

- **Predetermined consequences:** When setting boundaries, pair them with clear, predetermined consequences. If a boundary regarding respectful communication is violated, a consequence might be pausing the conversation until a

later time when both parties can engage more constructively.
- **Immediate response:** Time is of the essence. Addressing the breach promptly prevents escalation and underscores the seriousness with which you view these boundaries.
- **Consistent application:** Apply the same consequences for repeated violations. Inconsistency can send mixed signals, undermining the boundary's integrity.
- **Avoid participating in JADE:** JADE stands for Justify, Argue, Defend, Explain. Avoid these behaviors when enforcing boundaries. You are not required to justify or argue your need for your limits. A simple "As previously stated..." in retaliation to argument can suffice.

The goal here is not punitive but corrective, and aims to guide future interactions back within the bounds of respectful and constructive co-parenting.

Legal Recourse

Sometimes, despite your best efforts, a pattern of boundary violations emerges. This might necessitate stepping beyond personal enforcement strategies into the realm of legal intervention. This step is not taken lightly but is sometimes necessary to safeguard your well-being and establish enforceable limits. Here's what this might involve:

- **Documentation:** Keep a detailed record of boundary violations, noting dates, times, and the nature of the breach. This documentation can be invaluable in legal proceedings.
- **Legal consultation:** Seek advice from a legal professional skilled in family law, especially those with experience in

high-conflict co-parenting cases. They can offer guidance on the next steps, whether it involves mediation, court orders, or other legal remedies.
- **Formal complaints:** In cases of harassment or threats, filing a formal complaint may be necessary. This legal documentation can serve as a foundation for future legal actions if needed.

Navigating the legal system can be daunting, but it's sometimes a necessary path to enforce boundaries that are crucial for your and your children's well-being.

3.4 THE ROLE OF LEGAL BOUNDARIES AND ORDERS

Navigating co-parenting with a narcissist can sometimes require more than personal resolve and emotional strategies; it may necessitate the involvement of legal measures to ensure the safety and well-being of both you and your children. This could range from formalizing co-parenting agreements, to seeking restraining orders in extreme cases. This segment aims to shed light on utilizing legal avenues as a form of boundary enforcement, providing a shield against overreach and ensuring that the conditions of co-parenting are not just recommended, but required.

Exploring Legal Measures for Boundary Enforcement

Legal measures, such as restraining orders or specific mandates in custody agreements, can serve as formal, enforceable boundaries. These aren't tools to wield lightly, but are necessary measures when personal safety and the psychological well-being of your children is at stake. For instance, a restraining order might be necessary in cases of harassment or intimidation, while custody agreements can include clauses that limit or define communication and interaction, effectively setting legal boundaries that protect all parties involved.

- **Restraining Orders:** Applied in situations where there is a threat to personal safety, they detail the conditions the restrained party must adhere to.
- **Custody Agreements:** Can specify conditions regarding visitation, communication, and decision-making, providing a structured framework for co-parenting.

Here's when and how to consider legal boundaries:

- **Document violations:** Keep a log of boundary violations, especially those that impact the well-being of your children. This documentation can be crucial if legal action becomes necessary.
- **Seek legal counsel:** If violations persist or escalate, consult with a legal professional familiar with family law and, ideally, the dynamics of narcissistic behavior. They can guide you through the appropriate steps, whether these steps involve mediation or court action.
- **Formalize co-parenting agreements:** Legal agreements can specify boundaries around communication, visitation, and decision-making, providing a clear framework within which co-parenting must occur. These agreements can be enforced by the court which adds weight to your boundaries and further consolidates them as both serious and necessary.

Mediation and Arbitration

The adversarial nature of the courtroom can escalate conflicts, alternative dispute resolution methods like mediation and arbitration offer a more amicable route to resolving disputes. These settings encourage negotiation and compromise, which can be particularly beneficial in creating workable co-parenting arrangements.

- Mediation involves a neutral third party who helps both parents come to an agreement on contentious issues. It's a space where you can voice your concerns and work towards solutions without the formality and pressure of a courtroom.
- Arbitration, while more structured, allows a designated arbitrator to make decisions on disputed matters based on the evidence presented. This can be a faster, more efficient way to resolve specific legal issues.

Both methods require a willingness to compromise and prioritize the best interests of the children above the ongoing conflict with your ex.

The Importance of Legal Guidance

Working with attorneys and legal professionals who grasp the subtleties of narcissistic abuse is crucial. They can offer insights into the legal system's workings and how best to document and present your case. Their expertise not only aids in navigating the often-complex legal landscape, but also ensures that the measures you seek are aligned with your family's specific needs. This in turn will mean that these measures are more likely to be granted.

- **Choosing the Right Attorney:** Look for professionals with experience in family law, especially those who have handled cases involving high-conflict personalities or narcissistic abuse. Recommendations from support groups

or legal professionals can be invaluable in this search. In your initial consultation, assess the attorney's understanding of narcissistic behavior and their approach to high-conflict cases. Their strategy should align with your goals and the well-being of your children.
- **Legal Strategy:** Develop a strategy that reflects an understanding of narcissistic tactics, ensuring that your legal boundaries are robust, enforceable, and tailored to your unique situation.

Protective Orders

There are instances when the only viable option to ensure your and your children's safety is to seek a protective order against a narcissistic ex exhibiting threatening behavior. Understanding the criteria for obtaining such an order is crucial. Typically, you'll need to demonstrate a pattern of harassment, threats, or physical danger posed by your ex.

- Start by gathering any evidence of threatening messages, emails, or documented instances of harassment.
- Consult with a legal professional who can guide you through the process, ensuring that your application is both compelling and meets the legal requirements.

Obtaining a protective order is a significant step that can help deter further harassment and provide a measure of legal recourse should the behavior continue.

Empowering Yourself Through Legal Knowledge

Understanding the laws and precedents relevant to your situation empowers you to make informed decisions about your legal strategy. It also prepares you for all of the potential outcomes and helps you to anticipate and plan for various scenarios.

- **Research:** Take the time to learn about your local and state laws regarding custody, restraining orders, and other relevant legal measures.
- **Resources:** Utilize online tools like Nolo.com and LawHelp.org, legal aid societies such as the Legal Services Corporation, and workshops or community legal clinics to broaden your understanding of the legal aspects of co-parenting with a narcissist.

By taking these steps, you're not just protecting yourself and your children; you're laying down a foundation that demands respect and adherence to agreed-upon boundaries, enforced not by personal will but by the weight of the law. It's a way of affirming that while co-parenting with a narcissist presents unique challenges, there are structures and supports in place that can help you navigate this path, ensuring that your rights and well-being are upheld.

Self-Care in the Aftermath

The emotional toll of enforcing boundaries, especially when legal actions are involved, can be significant. It's essential, then, to prioritize self-care, allowing yourself time and space to recover and rebuild resilience. I understand that you probably once loved your ex, and therefore setting boundaries with them can be emotionally draining. My friend admitted that he will always love his narcissistic ex, but he knows he can't be in a relationship with her.

Although it is often overlooked, self-care is a critical boundary in the context of co-parenting with a narcissist. It's about setting limits, not just with your co-parent, but with yourself. These limits ensure that you don't deplete your resources or sacrifice your well-being in the face of ongoing stress. Here's how to prioritize self-care as a boundary:

- **Schedule self-care time:** Just as you would schedule work or children's activities, schedule regular time for self-care. This could be anything from quiet reading time, to exercise, or taking up hobbies that replenish your spirit like painting, or playing a musical instrument.
- **Learn to say no:** Saying no is a powerful boundary. It could mean declining additional demands on your time, or refusing to engage in conflict-instigating conversations with your co-parent.
- **Seek support:** An important part of self-care is recognizing when you need help, whether it's from friends, family, or mental health professionals. Support groups for those co-parenting with narcissistic ex-partners can also provide validation and strategies for coping.

Consider the following strategies for self-care:

- **Emotional outlets:** Writing in a journal, engaging in creative activities, or practicing mindfulness can help process emotions healthily.
- **Physical well-being:** Regular exercise, adequate sleep, and nourishing meals can bolster physical health, and provide you with the energy needed to face ongoing challenges.
- **Support systems:** Lean on friends, family, or support groups who understand your situation. Sharing

experiences and receiving encouragement can be incredibly affirming.
- **Fun:** Meet with your friends for a coffee, or take the kids on an exciting day out.

Taking care of yourself isn't a luxury—it's a vital component of navigating the challenging path of co-parenting with a narcissist. Establishing boundaries clearly, enforcing them consistently, and recognizing the role of legal measures and self-care in maintaining them, can transform the co-parenting experience from one of constant turmoil to one where stability and well-being can flourish, even in the most challenging of circumstances.

In wrapping up, this segment has illuminated the importance of understanding and utilizing legal measures as enforceable boundaries in co-parenting with a narcissist. From exploring legal options, to the significance of working with the right professionals, documenting interactions for legal purposes, and empowering yourself with knowledge, these steps are vital in ensuring your and your children's safety and well-being. It underscores the message that while the journey of co-parenting with a narcissist is fraught with challenges, there are mechanisms and systems in place designed to protect and support you. As we move forward, let us carry with us the understanding that legal boundaries, when thoughtfully applied and enforced, offer a framework within which healthier co-parenting dynamics can be nurtured and maintained, laying the groundwork for a future where respect and cooperation pave the way for the well-being of all involved.

3.5 TEACHING YOUR CHILDREN ABOUT BOUNDARIES

One of the most valuable lessons we can impart on our children is the understanding and respect for personal boundaries. This not only equips them with the tools to navigate their own relationships more effectively, but also reinforces the importance of mutual respect and personal space. Here's how to approach this critical subject with your children while ensuring the lessons are absorbed, understood, and applied.

Age-appropriate Discussions

Talking to your children about boundaries should be tailored to their age and level of understanding. It's akin to providing them with a map that matches their reading level; too complex, and they'll get lost; too simple, and they won't reach their destination.

- For younger children, the concept of boundaries can be introduced through the idea of personal space—like an invisible bubble around them that others need permission to enter.
- Older children and teenagers can handle more nuanced discussions. This might involve talking about emotional boundaries, such as the importance of saying no to situations that make them uncomfortable, and respecting others' rights to do the same.

The key is to make these discussions interactive. Ask questions, encourage them to share their thoughts, and use examples they can relate to, ensuring the concept of boundaries becomes a part of their thinking and not just another rule to follow. It may resonate with them if you use the example of when either you, or their sibling, goes into their bedroom without knocking first. This will help them to understand the effect that breaking boundaries has on others.

Modeling Respect for Boundaries

Children learn a lot through observation—watching how the adults in their lives interact can significantly influence their understanding of relationships. Demonstrating a healthy respect for others' boundaries is crucial. This might be as simple as knocking before entering their room, respecting their wishes not to discuss certain topics with friends or family, or acknowledging when they need time alone. By modeling this behavior, you're showing them that respecting boundaries is a fundamental part of healthy relationships, and setting a standard for how they should expect to be treated and how they should treat others.

Encouraging Autonomy

Empowering your children to set and communicate their own boundaries is a crucial step in fostering their sense of autonomy and respect for themselves and others. Encourage them to listen to their feelings and to speak up when something doesn't feel right. This could be related to their bodies, their possessions, or their emotions.

- Create opportunities for them to practice saying no in safe, low-stakes situations. For example, if they don't want to play a certain game or participate in an activity, support their decision and praise them for expressing their needs.
- Discuss scenarios they might encounter, like peer pressure or uncomfortable social situations, and role-play ways they can assert their boundaries. This not only prepares

them for real-life situations but also reinforces the idea that their boundaries are valid and should be respected.

Dealing with Violations

Despite their best efforts, there will be times when your children's boundaries are violated, either by peers, family members, or in their interactions with your ex-partner. Preparing them for how to respond to these situations is just as important as teaching them to set boundaries in the first place.

- Start with validation. Make sure they know that it's not their fault if someone disrespects their boundaries. Reinforce that they have the right to feel safe and respected always.
- Teach them to speak up. Encourage them to express clearly and firmly when a boundary has been crossed. Phrases like "I don't like it when you do that, please stop" or "I'm not comfortable with this" are simple yet powerful tools they can use.
- Advocate for themselves. In situations where the boundary violation is ongoing or involves an adult, like a teacher or even the other parent, discuss how they can seek help. This might mean coming to you, another trusted adult, or using school resources like a counselor.
- Reflect on the experience. After a boundary violation occurs, talk it through with them. Discuss what happened, how they felt, and what actions they took. This reflection can be empowering, helping them to process the event and reinforce their ability to handle similar situations in the future.

In imparting these lessons on boundaries, the ultimate goal is to instill in your children a deep-seated respect for themselves and others. It's about equipping them with the understanding and skills to navigate their relationships confidently, ensuring they know not just how to set and communicate their own boundaries but also how to respond when those boundaries are challenged. This education, grounded in respect, empathy, and personal strength, lays the foundation for their interactions and relationships, both now and in the future, encouraging a sense of self-respect and mutual understanding that will serve them well throughout their lives.

4

NURTURING EMOTIONAL SAFETY AND INTELLIGENCE

Imagine a world where every child can navigate their emotions with confidence and an understanding of the subtle nuances of their feelings and how to express them safely. This world isn't a far-off fantasy but a reality we can create, starting within our own homes. When co-parenting with a narcissist, where emotional manipulation can cloud the waters of communication, teaching our children about their emotional world becomes not just important but critical. It's about equipping them with the compass they need to steer through life's emotional landscapes, ensuring they can recognize changes and respond appropriately.

4.1 RECOGNIZING SIGNS OF EMOTIONAL MANIPULATION IN CHILDREN

Behavioral Changes

Noticing shifts in your child's behavior can be the first sign that something's amiss. Maybe your once bubbly child has become withdrawn, or your calm child seems unusually agitated. These changes might be subtle, like a reluctance to talk about time spent with the other parent or a sudden drop in school performance. Paying attention to these shifts is crucial. They're like the warning lights on a car's dashboard, signaling that it's time to look under the hood.

Emotional Intelligence

Teaching kids to name their emotions is like giving them a map of an uncharted territory. Start with the basics - happy, sad, angry, scared - and gradually introduce more nuanced emotions like frustration, disappointment, or nervousness. This can be done through everyday conversations, during story time by discussing characters' feelings, or through games designed to identify and express emotions. It's about making emotional language as natural to them as their native tongue, ensuring they can articulate what they're feeling and why. It would be helpful to watch the Disney film *Inside Out* with your child as it introduces the role each of our emotions plays in our daily lives.

Trusted Adults

Every child needs a go-to person, someone they can open up to without fear of judgment or reprimand. This could be you, a family member, a teacher, or a coach. Encourage your child to identify at least one trusted adult they feel comfortable talking to, ensuring they know it's okay to reach out for help when they're feeling overwhelmed or confused. It's like having a safety net, knowing it's there can make all the difference.

Professional Support

Sometimes, a professional can offer the support and guidance a child needs to navigate difficult emotions. If you notice signs of distress that linger or significantly impact your child's well-being, seeking help from a therapist who specializes in children and understands the dynamics of narcissistic families can be invaluable. They can provide a neutral, safe space for your child to explore their feelings and learn coping strategies.

Here's a list of online directories and resources where parents can find child therapists who specialize in emotional manipulation and high-conflict family dynamics:

Resource List for Child Therapists

1. **Psychology Today - Therapist Directory**
    - Psychology Today's directory allows you to search for child therapists by location and specialization. You can filter results for therapists experienced in family dynamics, emotional manipulation, and high-conflict situations.
2. **TherapyTribe - Family & Parenting Therapy**

- TherapyTribe offers a robust directory of licensed therapists, including those specializing in family counseling, child therapy, and high-conflict parenting situations.
3. **The National Child Traumatic Stress Network (NCTSN)**
    - The NCTSN has a directory of professionals specializing in trauma therapy for children affected by emotional manipulation and high-conflict families.
4. **GoodTherapy - Child and Adolescent Therapy**
    - GoodTherapy provides a searchable directory of licensed therapists who specialize in treating children and adolescents experiencing family-related stress, including high-conflict co-parenting situations.
5. **The American Association for Marriage and Family Therapy (AAMFT)**
    - The AAMFT offers a searchable directory of therapists specializing in family and marriage therapy, many of whom are experienced in working with high-conflict co-parenting and emotional manipulation.
6. **Child Mind Institute - Find a Therapist**
    - Child Mind Institute is a great resource for finding child therapists who specialize in behavioral issues stemming from family conflict and emotional manipulation.

7. **Parenting Apart - Co-Parenting Resources**
    - This resource provides a list of specialists who work with families dealing with co-parenting challenges, including therapists experienced in high-conflict and emotionally manipulative dynamics.
8. **Attachment and Trauma Network (ATN)**
    - ATN provides resources and directories for finding therapists who specialize in trauma-informed care, particularly in high-conflict family situations.
9. **The National Association of Social Workers (NASW)**
    - The NASW directory allows parents to find clinical social workers who specialize in child and family therapy, especially for high-conflict and emotionally manipulative environments.
10. **BetterHelp**
    - BetterHelp offers an online therapy platform where you can find licensed therapists, including those with experience in high-conflict parenting and child therapy.

Introducing children to the concept of emotional intelligence and helping them recognize the signs of emotional manipulation empowers them to navigate their relationships more effectively. It's about more than just making it through the day-to-day; it's about laying the foundation for lifelong emotional well-being and resilience.

4.2 FOSTERING OPEN COMMUNICATION WITH YOUR CHILDREN

Co-parenting with a narcissist can often leave our children caught in the middle, trying to find their footing. It's in these moments that the power of open communication shines brightest, acting as a guiding light for our children as they navigate their way through the complexities of their emotions and relationships. Open communication is not just about talking; it's about creating an environment where our children feel heard, understood, and valued.

Creating a Safe Space

Imagine a room filled with soft cushions, warm light, and the comforting aroma of home. This is the kind of safety we aim to replicate emotionally for our children—a haven where their thoughts and feelings can spill out without fear of judgment or repercussion. To cultivate this environment:

- Start with your demeanor; your body language, tone of voice, and even your breathing can signal to your child that this is a place of comfort and security.
- Reinforce this safety verbally. Remind them that they can share anything with you, and it will be received with love and understanding.
- Make this practice consistent. Safety isn't built in a day but through continuous effort and reassurance.

Active Listening

Active listening is an art form that requires us to fully immerse ourselves in our child's world. It's about more than just hearing their words, it's about understanding the emotions and experiences behind them. Here's how to master it:

- Give them your full attention. Turn off the TV, put away the phone, and eliminate any distractions that might take away from the moment.

- Use non-verbal cues to show that you're engaged. Nodding, maintaining eye contact, and leaning in are all signals that you're fully present.
- Reflect back what you've heard, not just to confirm your understanding but to show them their words have value. A simple "It sounds like you felt really left out when that happened" can go a long way.

Honesty with Boundaries

Maintaining honesty in our communication doesn't mean laying bare every adult concern or the intricate details of the co-parenting challenges. It's about finding the right balance—sharing truths in a way that's appropriate for their age and emotional maturity. To navigate this:

- Decide what information is necessary and beneficial for them to know. This could include changes in the co-parenting schedule or how certain decisions are made.
- Use language that's accessible to them, avoiding overly complex explanations or terminology that might confuse more than clarify.
- Be open about emotions, both theirs and yours, while making it clear that despite challenges, your love and commitment to their well-being remain unwavering.

Encouraging Questions

Curiosity is a natural part of childhood, and in the context of co-parenting, questions about the changes and challenges they observe or experience are inevitable. Encouraging this curiosity:

- Creates an opportunity for learning and understanding, turning potentially confusing situations into teachable moments.
- Helps them feel involved, showing that their thoughts and concerns matter in the family dynamic.
- Allows you to correct any misconceptions and reassure them about their security and the love both parents have for them.

To foster an environment where questions are welcomed:

- Prompt them gently if you sense there's something on their mind. A simple "Do you have any questions about what happened today?" can open the door.
- Respond with honesty, keeping in mind the guidelines for age-appropriate boundaries. If the answer is complex, break it down into simple parts they can grasp.
- Reassure them that no question is too small or silly to be asked. This not only aids their understanding but also strengthens their trust in you as a source of support and information.

In shaping a world where our children feel empowered to communicate openly, we give them the tools not only to express themselves but also to build relationships based on mutual respect and understanding. This open line of communication acts as a bridge over the tumultuous waters of co-parenting with a narcissist, guiding our children safely to the shores of emotional intelligence and resilience. Through active listening, honesty tempered with protective boundaries, and an encouragement of their innate curiosity, we lay down the stepping stones for our children to become not just effective communicators but also compassionate listeners and thinkers, capable of navigating the complex emotional landscapes of their lives with confidence and grace.

4.3 STRATEGIES FOR COUNTERACTING PARENTAL ALIENATION

Parental alienation, a complex and distressing phenomenon, occurs when one parent, often with narcissistic tendencies, systematically manipulates the child against the other parent. This manipulation not only strains the parent-child relationship but can also have long-term psychological impacts. Recognizing the signs of alienation early and addressing them proactively is crucial in mitigating its effects.

Understanding Parental Alienation

Identifying parental alienation involves observing changes in your child's perception and behavior towards you, which might not align with past experiences or the reality of your relationship. Signs include an inexplicable display of hostility, parroting the alienating parent's language, and unfounded rejection. The child might also show an unwarranted fear, disrespect, or lack of empathy towards the targeted parent, behaviors that are often out of character and instilled by the alienating parent's influence.

Strengthening the Parent-Child Bond

To effectively counteract parental alienation you will need to reinforce the bond between you and your child. This effort focuses on creating positive experiences and open lines of communication, devoid of the conflict involving the other parent. Here are practical steps to strengthen this crucial bond:

- **Prioritize Quality Time:** Engage in activities that your child enjoys, creating an environment where joy, rather than the ongoing conflict, takes center stage. These moments serve as a counterbalance to the negative narratives they might be hearing.
- **Listen Actively:** When your child shares feelings or thoughts, even those influenced by alienation tactics, listen without immediate correction or judgment. This approach helps maintain trust, showing your child they can be open with you without fear of reprisal.
- **Affirm Love and Commitment:** Regularly affirm your unconditional love for your child, emphasizing that your relationship with them is not contingent on their feelings or behavior towards you. This constant reassurance can be a beacon of stability in their often tumultuous emotional world.

Legal Interventions

When efforts to directly strengthen the parent-child relationship face obstacles due to ongoing alienation tactics, legal intervention might become necessary. This step involves:

- **Seeking Court-Ordered Therapy:** For both the child and the alienated parent, which can provide a neutral ground

for addressing misconceptions and rebuilding the relationship.
- **Modification of Custody Arrangements:** If alienation is severe and demonstrably harmful, seeking a modification in custody arrangements might be warranted. This process requires thorough documentation of alienation behaviors and their impact on the child.
- **Legal Advocacy for the Child:** In some cases, appointing an advocate or guardian ad litem for the child can ensure their voice is heard in legal proceedings, focusing on their best interests rather than the parents' conflict.

Support Networks

Creating a robust support system plays a pivotal role in mitigating the effects of parental alienation both for you and your children. This network can include:

- **Family and Friends:** Loved ones who understand the situation can offer emotional support and practical help, such as facilitating visits or providing a listening ear when you or your child need to talk.
- **Professional Counselors:** Professionals experienced in dealing with high-conflict co-parenting and parental alienation can offer strategies to cope and heal. They can also serve as an invaluable support system for your child, providing them with a safe space to express and work through their feelings.
- **Support Groups:** Joining groups, either in person or online, with others who have experienced similar challenges can be incredibly validating. These communities offer a sense of belonging and understanding that can be hard to find elsewhere, along

with shared strategies for overcoming the challenges of alienation.

Building and maintaining a strong parent-child bond, seeking appropriate legal recourse when necessary, and creating a nurturing support network are fundamental in counteracting the effects of parental alienation. These strategies not only help navigate the immediate challenges but also lay the groundwork for a healthier long-term relationship between you and your child, free from the shadow of alienation.

4.4 BUILDING RESILIENCE: HELPING YOUR CHILDREN BOUNCE BACK

In a world that constantly shifts beneath our feet, resilience stands as the cornerstone of emotional and psychological health. This is especially true for children navigating the complexities of co-parenting with a narcissist. Strengthening resilience in our children does more than prepare them for the challenges of today, it equips them with the fortitude to embrace life's uncertainties with confidence and poise. Here's a deeper exploration into teaching resilience, a trait that will serve them well into adulthood.

Promoting Problem-Solving Skills

Life is a series of puzzles, some straightforward, others complex and multifaceted. Teaching our children to approach problems with a critical eye is akin to giving them the keys to unlock these puzzles. Begin with simple challenges that they can relate to, and gradually increase the complexity as their skills grow. For instance, if they're struggling with a homework question, resist the urge to provide answers. Instead, guide them through the process of finding solutions on their own. You might ask probing questions that lead them to consider different angles or suggest they break the problem down into more manageable parts. This method not only enhances their problem-solving abilities but also instills a sense of accomplishment and independence.

- **Activity:** Set up a "problem of the week" that they can solve creatively, and offer rewards for innovative solutions.

Emphasizing Adaptability

Change is the only constant in life, and teaching our children to navigate these changes with a positive outlook can transform potential obstacles into opportunities for growth. Start by modeling adaptability in your daily life. When plans fall through or unexpected events occur, show them how to pivot gracefully rather than succumbing to frustration. Discuss the importance of being flexible and open to new experiences, and highlight how this mindset can lead to unexpected joys and discoveries. Encourage them to view change not as a threat but as a chance to learn and explore, laying the groundwork for a life rich in experiences and learning.

- **Reflection Exercise:** Encourage them to journal about a time when a change led to a positive outcome, focusing on the emotions and lessons learned. This might be starting a new year at school, or joining a new club.

Cultivating Self-Esteem

A child's self-esteem is like a plant that needs constant nurturing to grow. It thrives on positive affirmations, achievements, and unconditional love and support. Regularly point out their strengths and celebrate their efforts, regardless of the outcome. Encourage activities that align with their interests and abilities, providing a stage for them to shine and build confidence. Implement a daily affirmation ritual where you and your child express positive traits about yourselves and each other. This practice can fortify their self-worth, enabling them to face the world with confidence and resilience.

- **Affirmation Cards:** Create a deck of cards with positive affirmations and encouraging statements. Pick a card to discuss each morning, setting a positive tone for the day.

Supporting Social Connections

Humans are inherently social beings, and our relationships play a crucial role in our emotional well-being. For children, especially those caught in the crossfire of co-parenting dynamics, fostering healthy social connections is vital. Encourage them to cultivate friendships that bring joy and mutual respect. Involve them in activities or groups where they can meet peers with similar interests. Teach them the value of empathy, kindness, and support, guiding them to be the friend they wish to have. Additionally, connect them with supportive adults who can offer guidance and understanding, creating a network of positive influences that enrich their lives and bolster their resilience.

- **Social Skills Game Night:** Host a game night focusing on teamwork and communication, allowing them to practice social skills in a fun, low-pressure environment.

In guiding our children through the process of building resilience, we open doors to a world where challenges are met with courage, changes are embraced with optimism, and self-esteem is nurtured with love and support. We equip them with the skills to solve problems creatively, adapt to new situations with ease, believe in their own worth, and cherish the connections that make life meaningful. This preparation goes beyond the immediate hurdles of co-parenting with a narcissist, setting them on a path of emotional intelligence and resilience that will guide them through life's myriad of experiences.

4.5 THE IMPORTANCE OF A SUPPORTIVE HOME ENVIRONMENT

The home is more than a physical space. It transforms into a sanctuary of stability, comfort, and support, nurturing an atmosphere where children can thrive emotionally and psychologically. The creation of such an environment, amidst the unpredictability that often accompanies co-parenting challenges, is not just beneficial but necessary.

Creating a sanctuary of stability in the home begins with the conscious effort to shield the household from external chaos. This doesn't mean pretending challenges don't exist but rather ensuring that the home remains a constant in your children's lives, unaffected by the turmoil that might rage outside its walls. Strategies include:

- Keeping adult conversations about co-parenting challenges discreet, away from young ears that might not fully understand or might misinterpret the complexities of the situation.
- Maintaining a calm demeanor within the home, even when external pressures mount, providing a model of emotional regulation for your children.

Routines and rituals stand as pillars in the creation of this stable environment. They are the threads that weave through the fabric of daily life, providing predictability and a sense of security. These might include:

- A morning routine that starts the day on a positive note, perhaps with a shared breakfast or a moment of gratitude.
- Weekly rituals, like a family game night or a weekend nature walk, that children can look forward to, reinforcing the bond and shared joy among family members.

Encouraging an open dialogue about feelings and experiences within the home is crucial. It's about cultivating an atmosphere where emotions are not just acknowledged but are understood and respected. This open dialogue ensures:

- Regular check-ins where each family member can share highs and lows from their day, promoting emotional openness and mutual support.
- A policy of non-judgment, where feelings are validated, and solutions or comfort are offered, reinforcing the home as a safe space for emotional expression.

Positive reinforcement plays a key role in encouraging desired behaviors and building confidence. This approach, focusing on what children are doing right rather than where they might be falling short, includes:

- Praising efforts as well as achievements, highlighting the value of trying and the learning process itself.
- Recognizing and celebrating individual strengths, promoting a sense of self-worth and belonging within the family unit.

In crafting a home environment steeped in stability, routine, open communication, and positive reinforcement, we lay the groundwork for our children to navigate the complexities of their external world with confidence and emotional intelligence. It's about creating a haven that not only shelters but nurtures, allowing our children to grow, explore, and express themselves freely and fully.

As we close this exploration of the vital role a supportive home environment plays in the well-being of children co-parenting with a narcissistic ex, we're reminded of the power we hold. Through our actions, choices, and the atmosphere we cultivate, we have the ability to provide a foundation of stability, comfort, and emotional safety. This foundation not only supports our children's immediate needs but also contributes to their long-term emotional resilience and happiness. It's a testament to the strength and adaptability inherent in both parents and children, a strength that carries us forward, ready to face the next set of challenges with grace and determination.

SHARE YOUR EXPERIENCE, EMPOWER OTHERS

YOUR WORDS CAN BE A BEACON FOR THOSE IN NEED

"We make a living by what we get, but we make a life by what we give."

— WINSTON CHURCHILL

YOUR STORY CAN MAKE AN IMPACT

Every insight, strategy, and moment of strength you've gained from *Co-Parenting with a Narcissistic Ex* could mean the world to someone else struggling in a similar journey. By sharing your thoughts in a review, you're offering encouragement and guidance to others seeking to find peace, balance, and control in co-parenting.

WHY REVIEWS MATTER

Imagine a parent, exhausted and overwhelmed, searching for a way to manage life with a narcissistic ex. They need something that genuinely works—a book that provides understanding, tools, and hope. Your review could be the reason they find this resource and the clarity to move forward.

When you leave a review, you're showing others:

…there's a way to protect your peace,
…strategies for setting boundaries can be learned,
…their focus can shift back to their children,
…they can find relief and understanding.

MAKING A DIFFERENCE IS SIMPLE!

Writing a review takes just a minute, but its impact can reach far. Just scan the QR code below, or go to Amazon and share what this book has meant to you.

Thank you for being part of this journey and for helping others find their way through co-parenting challenges. Your words mean more than you know.

Warmly,

Casey Jordan

5

PRIORITIZING PERSONAL PEACE: THE SELF-CARE BLUEPRINT

Imagine standing at the edge of a serene lake. The water is calm, the air is fresh, and the only sounds are the gentle lapping of water against the shore and the distant call of a loon. This image mirrors the essence of self-care: building a tranquil sanctuary within ourselves that we can retreat to, especially when navigating the tumultuous waters of co-parenting with a narcissistic ex. It's a reminder that amidst the chaos, there exists a place of peace and rejuvenation. Self-care isn't just about bubble baths and spa days, it's about creating and maintaining this internal sanctuary, ensuring we can weather any storm with our well-being intact.

5.1 THE FUNDAMENTALS OF SELF-CARE

Understanding Self-Care

Self-care is the bedrock of our ability to function optimally, both as individuals and as parents. It's the act of attending to our physical, emotional, and mental health, not in a self-indulgent manner, but as a means to maintain our resilience in the face of stress. Think of it as the oxygen mask principle on airplanes: you need to secure your own mask before assisting others. In the context of co-parenting, this principle becomes even more critical, as the emotional toll can deplete your resources rapidly if not managed well.

Self-Care As A Priority

Shifting our perspective to view self-care as a necessity rather than a luxury is vital. It's easy to fall into the trap of thinking that taking time for self-care is selfish, especially when so many demands vie for our attention. However, neglecting self-care is akin to trying to fill cups from an empty pitcher - eventually, there's nothing left to give. By prioritizing our well-being, we ensure that we have the energy, patience, and emotional capacity to be the best parent possible.

Creating A Self-Care Plan

A self-care plan is your roadmap to maintaining balance and well-being. It addresses your physical, emotional, and mental health needs and outlines strategies for meeting them. Here's how to craft one:

- **Physical care:** List activities that contribute to your physical health, such as regular exercise, nutritious eating, and adequate sleep.
- **Emotional care:** Identify practices that support your emotional well-being. This could include journaling, engaging in hobbies, or spending time with loved ones.
- **Mental care:** Consider activities that help maintain your mental clarity and focus, such as meditation, reading, or learning a new skill.

Remember, your self-care plan is personal to you. What works for one person may not work for another, so tailor your plan to fit your needs and preferences.

Regular Assessment And Adaptation

Life is ever-changing, and so too are our needs. Regularly assessing and adapting your self-care plan ensures it remains relevant and effective. Set a monthly or quarterly review date to evaluate what's working, what isn't, and what might need to change. This process allows you to stay responsive to your evolving needs, ensuring your self-care practice grows with you.

To help you create a personalized and effective self-care routine, use the template below to guide you in addressing various aspects of your well-being and setting meaningful goals.

Self-Care Plan Template

1. Physical Well-Being

- **Exercise Routine**:
  - (e.g., daily walk, yoga class, strength training)

___

- **Nutrition Goals**:
  - (e.g., eat more fruits and vegetables, reduce sugar intake)

___

- **Sleep Schedule**:
  - (e.g., aim for 7-8 hours of sleep, establish a bedtime routine)

___

- **Health Check-Ups**:
  - (e.g., schedule regular doctor or dentist visits)

___

2. Emotional Well-Being

- **Coping Strategies for Stress**:
  - (e.g., journaling, deep breathing exercises, talking to a friend)

___

- **Activities That Bring Joy:**
  - (e.g., painting, reading, spending time in nature)

  _____

- **Emotional Support Network:**
  - (e.g., connect with friends, family, or a support group)

  _____

3. Mental Well-Being

- **Mindfulness Practices:**
  - (e.g., meditation, practicing gratitude, mindful eating)

  _____

- **Creative Outlets:**
  - (e.g., writing, drawing, playing an instrument)

  _____

- **Personal Development:**
  - (e.g., read a book, take an online course, set learning goals)

  _____

4. Social Well-Being

- **Connect with Others:**
  - (e.g., schedule time with friends, call a family member)

  _____

- **Set Boundaries**:
  - (e.g., limit time with toxic individuals, prioritize healthy relationships)

___

- **Join a Community or Group**:
  - (e.g., join a hobby group, attend local events)

___

5. Spiritual Well-Being (if applicable)

- **Practices to Nurture Your Spirit**:
  - (e.g., meditation, prayer, spending time in nature)

___

- **Personal Reflection**:
  - (e.g., journaling, daily gratitude practice)

___

6. Professional Well-Being

- **Work-Life Balance**:
  - (e.g., set boundaries for work hours, take regular breaks)

___

- **Career Goals**:
- (e.g., plan for a promotion, further education, or new career direction)

Self-Care Goals

- **Short-Term Goals**:

- **Long-Term Goals**:

Reflection

- **What's working well in your self-care routine?**

- **What needs improvement?**

In this section, we've laid the groundwork for understanding and implementing self-care as a critical component of navigating co-parenting with a narcissistic ex. From recognizing the essential nature of self-care to crafting a personalized care plan and adapting it over time, these strategies form the blueprint for maintaining personal peace and resilience. With this foundation, we move forward, exploring the facets of self-care that address emotional healing, physical health, social connections, and spiritual well-being, each contributing to the overall tapestry of our self-care practice.

5.2 EMOTIONAL SELF-CARE: HEALING FROM NARCISSISTIC ABUSE

In the wake of a relationship with a narcissist, we often find ourselves carrying wounds that are not visible to the eye but weigh heavily on the heart. The path to healing these emotional injuries is not always straightforward and requires a tender approach, focusing on nurturing our inner selves back to health. Here, we explore the steps necessary to mend the emotional scars left behind.

Recognizing Emotional Wounds

The first step toward healing is acknowledging the hurt. Emotional wounds from narcissistic abuse can manifest as lingering feelings of inadequacy, guilt, or a sense of lost identity. It's crucial to identify these feelings, not to dwell on them but to understand their origin. This process can be challenging, as it requires confronting painful truths about our experiences. Journaling can be a powerful tool in this journey, allowing for a private space where thoughts and feelings can be expressed freely, helping to untangle the complex emotions at play.

Seeking Professional Help

Navigating the aftermath of narcissistic abuse often necessitates guidance from those trained to deal with its complexities. Therapists or counselors specializing in narcissistic abuse possess the insights and strategies needed to address these unique challenges. They offer a supportive environment where healing can begin, anchored in understanding and validation. They can also introduce coping mechanisms tailored to your specific situation, ensuring the support provided aligns with your personal journey towards recovery.

Here is a directory of online resources and directories to help you find mental health professionals who specialize in narcissistic abuse and high-conflict relationships. Additionally, guidelines for selecting the right therapist are provided to ensure you find the best support for your needs.

1. Psychology Today - Therapist Directory

- Psychology Today offers an extensive therapist directory with filters for specialization, including narcissistic abuse and family dynamics. You can search by location, insurance, and specific issues like emotional manipulation or trauma.

2. GoodTherapy - Find a Therapist

- GoodTherapy allows users to find licensed therapists based on specific issues, including trauma and narcissistic abuse. Their directory emphasizes ethical therapy practices and offers a broad range of specializations.

3. BetterHelp - Online Therapy

- BetterHelp is an online platform that matches users with licensed therapists based on their needs. It includes professionals experienced in dealing with narcissistic relationships, emotional manipulation, and abuse recovery. Ideal for remote access.

---

4. TherapyTribe - Family & Narcissistic Abuse Therapists

- TherapyTribe connects individuals with therapists who specialize in family conflict, emotional abuse, and narcissistic relationships. Their directory includes therapists across a variety of specialties.

---

5. National Alliance on Mental Illness (NAMI) - Support Resources

- NAMI provides a directory of mental health professionals, support groups, and resources specifically designed for those dealing with trauma, family abuse, and high-conflict relationships.

---

6. DomesticShelters.org - Abuse Recovery Counselors

- A comprehensive resource for finding therapists who work with individuals recovering from narcissistic abuse and emotional manipulation. You can search for local counselors and find emergency services as well.

---

7. The American Psychological Association (APA) - Psychologist Locator

- The APA directory helps users find licensed psychologists by location and specialization. You can find therapists who work with narcissistic abuse, family counseling, and trauma recovery.

---

8. Trauma Recovery Institute

- Specializing in trauma therapy and narcissistic abuse recovery, the Trauma Recovery Institute provides online support and a directory of professionals equipped to handle high-conflict and emotionally abusive relationships.

Guidelines for Selecting the Right Therapist for Narcissistic Abuse Recovery:

1. **Look for Specialization in Trauma or Narcissistic Abuse**
   - Ensure that the therapist has specific experience with narcissistic abuse, emotional manipulation, or trauma recovery. Not all therapists are equipped to handle the unique dynamics of these situations.
2. **Verify Credentials**
   - Check the therapist's qualifications, certifications, and licensing. It's important to work with someone who has professional expertise in dealing with emotional abuse.
3. **Consider Therapy Style**
   - Look for therapists who use methods like Cognitive Behavioral Therapy (CBT), trauma-informed care, or EMDR (Eye Movement Desensitization and Reprocessing), which are often effective in treating trauma from narcissistic abuse.
4. **Ensure They Understand Narcissistic Personality Disorder**
   - Your therapist should have a solid understanding of narcissistic personality disorder (NPD) and its impact on relationships. This knowledge is critical for navigating complex dynamics.
5. **Seek a Supportive and Safe Environment**
   - Emotional safety is essential in therapy. Make sure your therapist is someone who provides a non-judgmental and supportive space for you to heal and grow.
6. **Check for Reviews and Recommendations**
   - If possible, look for testimonials or reviews from others who have gone through similar experiences. This can

help you find a therapist who truly understands your needs.

7. **Evaluate Accessibility and Flexibility**
   - Depending on your needs, online therapy platforms like BetterHelp can provide flexibility, while others may prefer in-person sessions. Ensure the therapist's location, hours, and format align with your lifestyle.

By using these resources and guidelines, you can find a therapist who understands the complexities of narcissistic abuse and will support you on your path to recovery.

Building Emotional Resilience

The road to recovery is also about building the resilience needed to face future challenges without the past overshadowing your present. Techniques such as mindfulness and emotional regulation play a pivotal role in this process. Mindfulness encourages living in the moment, reducing the power of past traumas over your current state of mind. Emotional regulation strategies, such as deep breathing exercises or meditation, can help manage the intensity of emotions, providing a sense of control over reactions and feelings.

When co-parenting with a narcissistic ex, moments of distress can arise unexpectedly. This mindfulness exercise is designed to help you center your thoughts and emotions, providing a sense of calm and clarity during challenging times.

Mindfulness Exercise: Centering Your Mind and Emotions

1. Find a Quiet Space

- **Action**: Sit comfortably in a quiet place where you won't be disturbed for a few minutes.
- **Tip**: It could be a cozy corner in your home, a peaceful spot in a park, or even your car before or after a drop-off.

2. Assume a Comfortable Posture

- **Action**: Sit with your back straight but relaxed, feet flat on the ground, and hands resting gently in your lap.
- **Tip**: You can also lie down if that feels more comfortable.

3. Focus on Your Breathing

- **Action**: Close your eyes and take a deep breath in through your nose for a count of four.
- **Breathing Technique**:
  - **Inhale**: Slowly breathe in for a count of four.
  - **Hold**: Hold your breath for a count of four.
  - **Exhale**: Gently breathe out through your mouth for a count of six.
  - **Repeat**: Do this breathing cycle five times.

4. Body Scan Meditation

- **Action**: Shift your focus to different parts of your body, starting from your toes and moving up to your head.
- **Steps**:
  - **Toes and Feet**: Notice any sensations, tension, or relaxation.

- **Legs and Hips**: Observe how they feel without trying to change anything.
- **Torso and Shoulders**: Release any tightness or stress you might be holding.
- **Arms and Hands**: Feel the weight and movement.
- **Neck and Head**: Relax your jaw, soften your gaze, and let go of any lingering thoughts.

5. Acknowledge Your Emotions

- **Action**: Bring your attention to your current emotional state.
- **Technique**:
  - **Identify**: Name the emotion you're feeling (e.g., frustration, anxiety, sadness).
  - **Accept**: Acknowledge the emotion without judgment. It's okay to feel this way.
  - **Release**: Imagine the emotion gently flowing out of you with each exhale.

6. Visualize Calmness

- **Action**: Picture a place where you feel safe and calm. It could be a beach, a forest, or any serene environment.
- **Technique**:
  - **Details**: Focus on the details—sounds, sights, smells.
  - **Immerse**: Allow yourself to fully immerse in this peaceful setting for a few minutes.

7. Affirmations for Strength

- **Action**: Silently repeat positive affirmations to reinforce your inner strength.

- **Examples**:
  - "I am calm and centered."
  - "I handle challenges with grace."
  - "My well-being is important."

8. Gently Return to the Present

- **Action**: Slowly bring your awareness back to your surroundings.
- **Steps**:
  - **Movement**: Wiggle your fingers and toes.
  - **Stretch**: Stretch your arms and legs if needed.
  - **Open Eyes**: When you're ready, open your eyes and take a final deep breath.

9. Reflect and Journal (Optional)

- **Action**: Take a moment to jot down any thoughts or feelings that arose during the exercise.
- **Benefit**: Helps in processing emotions and tracking your mindfulness progress.

Tips for Effective Practice

- **Consistency**: Incorporate this exercise into your daily routine, even if only for a few minutes each day.
- **Flexibility**: Use this exercise whenever you feel overwhelmed, not just during peak distress moments.
- **Patience**: Mindfulness is a skill that develops over time. Be patient with yourself as you practice.

- **Environment**: Create a calming environment by dimming lights, playing soft music, or using aromatherapy if it helps you relax.

By regularly practicing this mindfulness exercise, you can build resilience and maintain emotional balance, making co-parenting with a narcissistic ex more manageable and fostering a healthier environment for both you and your children.

Self-Compassion

At the heart of healing lies self-compassion, a gentle reminder that you deserve kindness and understanding from yourself as much as from others. It's about forgiving yourself for any perceived mistakes or for simply being in a relationship with a narcissist. Regret is an unhealthy emotion, remember not to blame yourself for falling for a narcissist's charm, and without that relationship you never would have had your children/child. Self-compassion acknowledges that healing is not a linear process and that setbacks are part of the journey. It encourages a dialogue with oneself that is nurturing rather than critical, recognizing the strength it takes to heal and move forward.

Take a moment to reflect on these questions and allow yourself the space to explore your emotions without judgment. Use these prompts to practice self-compassion and offer yourself the same kindness you would extend to someone you care about.

1. **"What would I say to a friend in my situation?"**
    - Imagine a close friend is going through the same experience. How would you comfort and support them? Write down the words of encouragement you

would offer them, and then apply those same sentiments to yourself.
2. **"How can I show myself kindness today?"**
    - Reflect on small acts of kindness you can offer yourself. Whether it's taking a break, engaging in a hobby, or simply giving yourself permission to rest, note what would help nurture your well-being.
3. **"What strengths have I shown throughout this journey?"**
    - Think about the resilience, courage, or patience you've demonstrated during difficult times. Acknowledge the inner strength you've used to navigate your path.
4. **"In what ways am I healing, even if it feels slow?"**
    - Healing isn't always visible or fast, but it happens in small, meaningful ways. Reflect on the progress you've made, no matter how small, and celebrate those steps forward.
5. **"What can I forgive myself for today?"**
    - We often hold ourselves accountable for things beyond our control. What mistakes or regrets can you release, knowing you are human and deserving of compassion?
6. **"How can I remind myself that setbacks are part of growth?"**
    - Reflect on any recent setbacks and view them through the lens of growth. How can these experiences teach you and help you move forward, rather than hold you back?

These prompts are designed to help you cultivate a nurturing, compassionate relationship with yourself as you continue your healing journey. Use them as a tool to check in with yourself and to reinforce the kindness and understanding you deserve.

In focusing on these aspects of emotional self-care, we gradually mend the wounds inflicted by narcissistic abuse. This process is deeply personal and unfolds at its own pace. It's a testament to the human spirit's resilience and capacity for renewal, guided by the light of self-awareness, professional support, emotional resilience, and, most importantly, self-compassion. Through these practices, we not only heal but also rediscover our strength and joy, embarking on a new chapter marked by inner peace and empowerment.

5.3 PHYSICAL SELF-CARE: THE ROLE OF EXERCISE AND NUTRITION

In the realm of self-care, the emphasis often leans heavily towards the mental and emotional aspects, leaving the physical component as an afterthought. Yet, the interconnection between body and mind is so profound that neglecting physical well-being can significantly hamper our ability to cope with stress and recover from emotional turmoil. This section looks at how incorporating regular exercise, mindful nutrition, sleep hygiene, and routine health checks into our lives can act as powerful allies in our quest for balance and wellness.

Exercise as Stress Relief

The benefits of regular physical activity extend far beyond the visible. Engaging in exercise releases endorphins, these are natural mood lifters that can reduce stress and enhance well-being. It's a tool that not only strengthens the body but also clears the mind, offering a much-needed respite from the mental strain of co-parenting challenges. Whether it's a brisk walk, a yoga session, or a more intense workout, the key is consistency and finding joy in the movement. Here are a few ways to integrate exercise into daily routines:

- **Set Realistic Goals:** Start with manageable activities that fit into your schedule. Even ten minutes a day can make a difference.
- **Find Activities You Enjoy:** Exercise shouldn't feel like a chore. Whether it's dancing, cycling, or swimming, choose activities that bring you joy.
- **Make It Social:** Involve friends or join a class. This adds a layer of social interaction, enhancing the stress-relieving benefits of the exercise.

Nutrition for Mental Health

The adage "You are what you eat" holds true for our mental and emotional health as much as it does for our physical well-being. A balanced diet rich in fruits, vegetables, whole grains, and lean proteins can provide the nutrients essential for maintaining energy levels, improving mood, and supporting overall health. Here are some guidelines for mindful eating:

- **Hydration:** Keeping hydrated is crucial. Water helps to flush out toxins and keeps the brain functioning optimally.
- **Mindful Eating:** Pay attention to what and how you eat. Enjoy your food, savor each bite, and listen to your body's hunger and fullness cues.
- **Limit Processed Foods:** High sugar and processed foods can lead to energy crashes and mood swings. Opt for whole foods to keep your energy and mood more stable.

Sleep Hygiene

Quality sleep is as vital to our health as diet and exercise. It's during sleep that the body and mind recover from the day's stresses, making good sleep hygiene practices a critical component of physical self-care. A restful night involves more than just the number of hours asleep, it also includes creating the right environment and habits to promote sound sleep. Consider these tips:

- **Establish a Routine:** Going to bed and waking up at the same time every day help regulate your body's internal clock.
- **Create a Restful Environment:** Make your bedroom a sanctuary for sleep. Keep it cool, dark, and quiet.
- **Limit Screen Time:** The blue light emitted by screens can interfere with your ability to fall asleep. Try reading a book or practicing relaxation exercises before bed instead.

Routine Health Checks

Regular check-ups with healthcare professionals play a significant role in the early detection and prevention of health issues. Stress can have a tangible impact on our physical health, and routine medical checks can help in identifying and addressing any stress-related conditions before they escalate. Here's how to stay on top of your health:

- **Schedule Annual Check-ups:** Make appointments for regular physical exams, dental check-ups, and any other necessary screenings.
- **Listen to Your Body:** Pay attention to any signs that might indicate stress is affecting your physical health, such as headaches, digestive issues, or changes in sleep patterns.

- **Stay Informed:** Keep yourself informed about your health status and any potential risks. Knowledge is power, and understanding your health allows for better management of stress and its physical manifestations.

Incorporating these aspects of physical self-care into our daily lives requires dedication and mindfulness. Yet, the rewards — increased energy, improved mood, and a stronger, more resilient body — are well worth the effort. It's a testament to the power of taking care of our physical selves as a pathway to achieving a balanced and fulfilling life, even in the face of challenging co-parenting dynamics.

5.4 SOCIAL SELF-CARE: BUILDING A SUPPORT NETWORK

In the tapestry of self-care practices, weaving a robust social fabric stands out as a critical element. After periods of isolation, particularly those experienced during challenging co-parenting dynamics, the act of reaching out and rekindling connections with friends, family, and supportive communities is not just healing but revitalizing. It's akin to opening the windows after a long winter, allowing fresh air and sunlight to cleanse and rejuvenate the space within.

Reconnecting with Others

The path to reconnecting may seem daunting, especially after periods of withdrawal that often accompany emotional upheaval. Yet, the rewards of re-establishing these connections are immense. Start small, perhaps with a message or call to someone you trust and miss. It's about taking those first steps, however tentative, towards rebuilding your social landscape. These reconnections can serve as a reminder that you're not alone, providing a sense of belonging and comfort.

- Consider scheduling regular meet-ups, even if it's just a virtual coffee chat, to gradually rebuild your social stamina and presence.
- Initiate conversations that go beyond the surface, allowing for a genuine exchange of thoughts and feelings. This depth can foster a stronger sense of connection and understanding.

Setting Boundaries in Relationships

As you venture into the social world, being mindful of setting healthy boundaries is paramount. It helps in managing your energy and ensuring interactions remain positive and supportive. Think of boundaries as your personal guidelines for what you consider acceptable and beneficial in your interactions with others.

- Clearly communicate your needs and limits to friends and family. This may involve expressing when you need space or specifying topics you're not comfortable discussing.
- Pay attention to how different interactions make you feel. If certain connections leave you feeling drained or upset, it might be time to reassess their place in your life.

Seeking out Support Groups

There's a unique strength found in shared experiences. Support groups, whether in-person or online, offer a space where empathy and understanding flow freely, grounded in the common challenges and triumphs of their members. The benefits of finding a group that resonates with your experiences are manifold:

- Discovering you're not alone in your struggles can be incredibly affirming and empowering.
- Sharing strategies and insights with individuals facing similar situations can offer new perspectives and coping mechanisms.
- Witnessing the resilience and growth of others can serve as a beacon of hope and inspiration for your own journey.

Cultivating New Relationships

As you navigate the process of social self-care, the opportunity to cultivate new relationships emerges. These connections, built on mutual respect and understanding, can enrich your life in ways you might not have anticipated. Here are some tips for fostering healthy, fulfilling relationships:

- Explore new interests or hobbies as a way to meet like-minded individuals. Common interests can serve as a strong foundation for a lasting friendship.
- Approach new relationships with openness and curiosity. Listen actively and share about yourself with honesty, allowing for a genuine connection to develop.
- Be patient. Deep, meaningful relationships take time to grow. Allow these new connections the space and time they need to flourish.

In the realm of self-care, tending to our social well-being is as crucial as nurturing our physical, emotional, and mental health. The process of reconnecting with loved ones, setting healthy boundaries, finding solace in support groups, and welcoming new relationships into our lives not only strengthens our social fabric but also reinforces our resilience against life's challenges. It reminds us of the power of community and connection, offering a wellspring of support, understanding, and companionship on which we can draw in times of need. Through these social self-care practices, we fortify our capacity for joy, growth, and fulfillment, enriching our journey with the warmth and vibrancy of shared human experience.

5.5 SPIRITUAL SELF-CARE: FINDING PEACE AND PURPOSE

Within the walls we build around our daily lives to keep chaos at bay, there's often a neglected space that yearns for nourishment—the spiritual self. It's in this realm where we seek and find tranquility and a deeper connection to the world around us. Spiritual self-care is an invitation to explore the dimensions of our being that transcend the physical and emotional, guiding us to a place of inner peace and purpose.

Exploring Spirituality

Spirituality transcends specific beliefs or practices; it's a personal quest for meaning and connection with something greater than ourselves. This exploration can take myriad forms, from organized religion to personal meditation, nature walks, or the study of philosophical texts. It's about finding paths that resonate with your soul, offering a sense of belonging and understanding in the vast tapestry of existence. Start small—dedicate a few moments each day to sit in silence, light a candle with an intention, or read passages from texts that inspire you. The goal is to create a habit that draws you closer to the inner peace and wisdom you seek.

Meditation and Mindfulness

Meditation and mindfulness stand as pillars in the practice of spiritual self-care, offering tools to quieten the mind and anchor the self in the present moment. These practices teach us to observe our thoughts and emotions without judgment, creating a state of calm awareness amidst life's storms. Begin with just a few minutes a day, focusing on your breath or a simple mantra, and gradually increase the time as you become more comfortable with the practice. You might find that these moments of stillness become a sanctuary, a place to recharge and realign with your core values and goals.

- **Mindfulness Exercise:** Try incorporating mindfulness into routine activities, such as eating or walking. Pay close attention to the sensations and experiences of the moment—the texture of your food, the feel of the ground under your feet. This practice can transform mundane tasks into rich, fulfilling experiences.

Connecting with Nature

Nature, in its infinite variety and beauty, offers a profound source of spiritual nourishment. The act of spending time outdoors—be it a forest, a local park, or your backyard—can help dissolve feelings of isolation or disconnect, reminding us of our place within the larger web of life. Make a habit of observing the natural world around you, whether it's watching birds from a window, tending to a garden, or walking beneath the trees. These connections can serve as powerful reminders of the beauty and resilience inherent in both the world and ourselves.

- **Nature Journal:** Keep a journal of your experiences in nature. Note the changes in the seasons, the plants and animals you encounter, and the feelings these observations evoke. This record can become a source of inspiration and reflection, deepening your connection to the natural world.

Finding Purpose in Adversity

Adversity, though challenging, carries with it the seeds of growth and transformation. It's in the crucible of difficult experiences that we often discover a deeper sense of purpose and direction. Reflect on the challenges you've faced, particularly in the context of co-parenting with a narcissistic ex, and consider the lessons and strengths you've gained. How have these experiences shaped your understanding of yourself and your values? Embracing the growth that comes from adversity can lead to a profound sense of purpose, guiding your actions and decisions from a place of wisdom and compassion.

- **Reflection Exercise:** Write about a particularly challenging period in your life, focusing on what you learned from the experience. How did it change your perspective or priorities? How can you use these insights to inform your path forward?

In weaving the practices of spiritual self-care into the fabric of our lives, we open ourselves to a world of inner peace, purpose, and connection. This journey invites us to explore the depths of our being, to find solace in stillness, to reconnect with the natural world, and to draw strength and wisdom from the challenges we've overcome. It's a path that leads not just to self-discovery but to a profound engagement with the world around us, enriched by a sense of belonging and understanding that transcends the everyday.

As we wrap up this exploration of spiritual self-care, we carry with us the understanding that caring for the spirit is not an isolated task but an integral part of our overall well-being. It complements and deepens the practices of emotional, physical, and social self-care, weaving together a holistic approach to wellness that sustains us through the trials and triumphs of life. With this foundation, we move forward, equipped not only to navigate the complexities of our circumstances but to thrive within them, guided by a renewed sense of purpose and a deep well of inner peace.

6

FINANCIAL INDEPENDENCE AND RECOVERY

Imagine standing in the kitchen, trying to separate an intricately entwined bundle of necklaces. Each chain represents a different aspect of your life entangled with your narcissistic ex, especially finances. The process is delicate, requiring patience and a steady hand to untangle each link without causing damage. This is what it feels like to untangle your financial ties with a narcissist. It's intricate, sometimes frustrating, but absolutely necessary for regaining independence and peace.

6.1 UNTANGLING FINANCIAL TIES WITH A NARCISSIST

Assessment of Financial Entanglement

Start by laying out all financial documents on the table - bank statements, bills, loan documents, and anything else that ties you together. Assessing the extent of your financial entanglement is like taking stock of what's in the pantry before planning a big meal. You need to know what ingredients you have, their quantities, and what's expired. Similarly, understanding your financial landscape is crucial. It's about knowing what accounts you share, what debts are in both of your names, and what assets are jointly owned. This step is foundational, offering a clear picture of what needs to be addressed.

Seeking Professional Advice

Now, imagine you're preparing a gourmet dish for the first time. You'd likely seek guidance from a chef or a detailed recipe. Similarly, navigating financial separation requires expertise. Consulting with financial advisors and lawyers who specialize in divorce and financial separation is crucial. They can provide tailored advice on how to protect your assets, split shared debts, and navigate the legal complexities of financial separation. Their expertise is your recipe for successfully untangling the complex web of finances entwined with your narcissistic ex.

Use this checklist to ensure you're fully prepared for your consultation with a financial advisor or lawyer. Having these documents and details ready will help streamline the process and provide a comprehensive picture of your financial entanglement.

---

1. Bank Account Information

- ☐ **Joint Checking and Savings Account Statements**
- ☐ **Individual Account Statements**
- ☐ **Details of any online banking accounts or shared access**

2. Credit Cards and Loans

   ☐ Credit Card Statements (Joint and Individual)
   ☐ Loan Documents (Personal, Auto, Student, etc.)
   ☐ Mortgage Documents
   ☐ Any Other Debts (e.g., family loans, medical bills)

3. Investments and Retirement Accounts

   ☐ Investment Portfolio Statements (Stocks, Bonds, Mutual Funds)
   ☐ Retirement Accounts (401(k), IRA, Pension)
   ☐ Certificates of Deposit (CDs)

4. Property and Asset Information

   ☐ Deeds for Jointly Owned Property (e.g., house, land)
   ☐ Valuations of Property (Real Estate, Vehicles, etc.)
   ☐ Titles for Vehicles (Cars, Boats, etc.)
   ☐ Ownership Documents for Other Major Assets (e.g., jewelry, artwork)

5. Income and Employment Records

   ☐ Pay Stubs (Yours and Your Ex's, if applicable)
   ☐ Tax Returns for the Last 3–5 Years
   ☐ Records of Bonuses, Commissions, or Additional Income
   ☐ Any Documentation of Unreported Income (if known)

6. Business and Self-Employment Documents

- ☐ Business Ownership Documents
- ☐ Profit and Loss Statements for Joint or Individual Businesses
- ☐ Business Tax Returns
- ☐ Assets Owned by a Business (Vehicles, Equipment, etc.)

7. Legal Documents

- ☐ Prenuptial/Postnuptial Agreements
- ☐ Separation Agreement (if already in place)
- ☐ Divorce Papers or Ongoing Legal Proceedings Documents

8. Insurance Policies

- ☐ Life Insurance Policies (Joint and Individual)
- ☐ Homeowners or Renters Insurance
- ☐ Health, Disability, and Auto Insurance Policies
- ☐ Statements of Insurance Premiums

9. Child-Related Financials

- ☐ Child Support Payments (Received or Paid)
- ☐ Education Savings Plans (529 Plans, etc.)
- ☐ Expenses for Childcare, Education, or Extracurricular Activities

10. Miscellaneous

- ☐ Shared Utility Bills (Electric, Water, Internet, etc.)
- ☐ Memberships or Subscriptions (Gym, Magazines, etc.)

☐ Other Financial Obligations (Alimony, Family Loans)

Additional Information to Gather:

- Financial Power of Attorney Documents
- Details of Any Trusts or Inheritances
- Password and Access Information for Joint Accounts

By gathering these documents and organizing them before your consultation, you'll ensure that your financial advisor or lawyer has all the necessary information to guide you effectively through the process of financial separation.

With a clear understanding of your financial situation and professional advice in hand, it's time to build a new budget. Imagine this as drawing the blueprints for a house where you'll soon live. This budget is your blueprint, outlining how you'll allocate your resources moving forward. Start by listing all sources of income and expenses, identifying areas where adjustments are necessary to ensure financial stability. This could mean cutting back on non-essential spending or finding ways to increase your income. The aim is to create a budget that supports your current needs while laying the groundwork for future financial independence.

To help you get started, use the budget template below as a practical tool to organize your finances. By tracking your income, expenses, and savings, you'll gain better control over your financial landscape and make informed decisions about where adjustments are needed. This step-by-step approach will guide you toward creating a sustainable financial plan that aligns with your goals for independence and stability.

Budget Template

Category	Planned Amount	Actual Amount	Difference
Income			
- Salary			
- Additional Income			
Fixed Expenses			
- Rent/Mortgage			
- Utilities			
- Car Payment			
- Insurance			
- Childcare			
Variable Expenses			
- Groceries			
- Entertainment			
- Transportation			
- Medical Expenses			
Savings			
Other			

Protecting Assets and Credit

In the final stretch of untangling, it's paramount to safeguard what's yours and secure your financial future. Think of it as weatherproofing your house before a storm hits. Protecting your assets might involve removing your ex's access to joint bank accounts or ensuring property titles are in your correct name. When it comes to credit, start by reviewing your credit report for any inaccuracies or joint accounts that could impact your score. If necessary, open new accounts in your name only, and set up alerts to monitor your credit for any unauthorized activities. These steps are not just about immediate protection but also about laying a foundation for a financially secure future, free from unwelcome surprises.

For many, navigating the financial aftermath of a relationship with a narcissist feels overwhelming. Yet, with a methodical approach - assessing the extent of financial entanglement, seeking professional advice, crafting a budget and financial plan, and taking steps to protect assets and credit - it's entirely possible to untangle the knots and lay the groundwork for a stable, independent financial future. Just like separating those intertwined necklaces, the task requires patience, precision, and sometimes, the guidance of experts, but the sense of freedom and accomplishment waiting on the other side makes the effort undeniably worth it.

6.2 STRATEGIES FOR FINANCIAL EMPOWERMENT

Gaining control over your finances, especially after untangling them from a relationship with a narcissistic partner, is much like learning to navigate a new city without a map. At first, the streets seem unfamiliar and the destinations far-flung, but with time, practice, and a bit of guidance, you start to find your way around, discovering shortcuts and points of interest that weren't apparent at the outset. This section aims to equip you with the skills and knowledge to not only navigate but thrive in your new financial landscape.

Empowerment through Education

The first step on this road is empowering yourself with knowledge. Just as a gardener needs to understand the soil and climate to cultivate a thriving garden, you need to grasp the basics of personal finance, investment, and economic self-sufficiency. This could mean enrolling in online courses, attending workshops, or simply dedicating time each day to read books or articles on financial topics. Think of this as laying the foundation of your financial house, ensuring it's strong enough to support your goals and withstand future storms.

- **Educational Platforms:** Look for platforms offering courses on personal finance and investing, many of which are free or low-cost.
- **Reading List:** Compile a list of must-read books and articles that cover a wide range of financial topics, from budgeting basics to investment strategies. Goodreads is a great place to search for books by their subject and topic.

Building Financial Skills

With a solid foundation of knowledge, the next step is to build upon it by developing practical financial management skills. This is akin to a chef mastering the techniques of chopping, sautéing, and baking, each skill is essential in creating a successful dish. For you, these skills include budgeting effectively, understanding how to save for both short-term needs and long-term goals, and learning the basics of investing to grow your wealth over time.

- **Budgeting Apps:** Utilize apps that help you to track spending and set budgets, giving you a clear picture of where your money is going each month.
- **Savings Strategies:** Explore different savings strategies, such as setting aside a fixed percentage of your income each month or using automated transfers to savings accounts.

Creating Multiple Income Streams

Relying on a single source of income is like planting an entire garden with just one type of seed - if it fails to thrive, you're left with nothing. Diversifying your income, on the other hand, ensures that if one stream dries up, you have others to rely on. This might involve turning a hobby into a side business, investing in dividend-paying stocks, or renting out a property. Each new stream adds another layer of financial security, protecting you against the unpredictability of life.

- **Side Hustle Ideas:** List potential side hustles that align with your skills and interests, providing a starting point for creating additional income.
- **Investment Opportunities:** Research low-risk investment options that can generate passive income, such as real estate or dividend stocks.

Financial Goal Setting

Finally, setting clear financial goals gives you destinations to aim for on your journey. Without goals, it's easy to wander aimlessly, spending without purpose and saving without motivation. Start by identifying what's most important to you, whether it's buying a home, funding your child's education, or securing a comfortable retirement. Then, break these down into achievable steps, setting both short-term targets (saving for a vacation) and long-term objectives (building a retirement fund). This approach not only keeps you focused but also provides a sense of achievement as you tick off each goal along the way.

- **Goal Tracker:** Use a journal or an app to track your progress towards each financial goal. Celebrate milestones to maintain motivation.
- **Financial Planning Sessions:** Schedule regular check-ins with yourself to review and adjust your goals as needed,

ensuring they continue to align with your evolving priorities and circumstances.

In this endeavor to achieve financial empowerment, the path is neither straight nor without obstacles. However, with each step taken—be it through gaining knowledge, honing skills, diversifying income, or setting goals—you not only move closer to your financial destinations but also build a landscape rich with opportunity and security. These strategies, tools, and practices serve as your compass, guiding you through the complexities of personal finance and towards a future where financial independence and peace of mind are not just dreams but tangible realities.

6.3 NAVIGATING CHILD SUPPORT AND ALIMONY CHALLENGES

In the wake of separating from a narcissistic partner, the road to financial independence often involves the intricate process of navigating child support and alimony. This task demands not just a keen understanding of one's legal rights but also the finesse to negotiate terms that uphold the well-being and stability of all involved, especially the children.

Understanding Legal Entitlements

The initial step in this process requires a clear grasp of what the law stipulates regarding child support and alimony. Typically, child support payments are determined by a standard formula that takes into account the income of both parents, the needs of the child, and the custody arrangement. Alimony, however, varies greatly and is influenced by factors such as the length of the marriage, the standard of living during the marriage, and each partner's earning capacity.

- **Resources for Understanding:** Familiarizing oneself with these laws is crucial. Many jurisdictions offer calculators or guidelines online to help estimate potential payments. Additionally, consulting with a legal expert can provide insight into how these laws apply to your specific situation.

Negotiating Fair Arrangements

Once you're armed with knowledge about your entitlements, the next phase involves negotiating terms that are fair and sustainable. It's akin to navigating a negotiation for a significant purchase, where both parties seek a deal that reflects their needs and contributions.

- **Mediation as a Tool:** Often, mediation can serve as an effective avenue for reaching an agreement. A neutral third party can help facilitate discussions, ensuring that the focus remains on the needs of the children and the fairness of the terms.
- **Preparation is Key:** Before entering negotiations, prepare a detailed outline of your financial needs and expectations. This preparation can serve as a roadmap, guiding the conversation and helping to ensure that the final agreement reflects the best interests of all parties.

Enforcing Payments

Despite the best efforts to reach amicable agreements, there are instances when a narcissistic ex might delay or evade financial responsibilities. In such cases, several avenues exist to enforce these obligations.

- **State Enforcement Agencies:** Most jurisdictions have agencies dedicated to enforcing child support and alimony orders. These agencies can take various actions, such as garnishing wages, seizing tax refunds, or even pursuing legal action against delinquent payers.
- **Legal Recourse:** For persistent non-compliance, returning to court might be necessary. The court can impose penalties, alter the narcissistic ex's custody rights, or take other measures to ensure compliance.

Adjusting to Financial Changes

As child support and alimony agreements are put into place and payments begin to flow, a period of adjustment follows. This adjustment is not just financial but also emotional, as it often represents a significant shift in the dynamics of post-separation life.

- **Budgeting for the New Normal:** With child support and alimony figures in hand, revisiting and adjusting your budget is crucial. This might mean reallocating funds to different areas, saving for future needs, or even reevaluating financial goals.
- **Staying Flexible:** Life is in constant flux, and the needs of children evolve, incomes change, and unexpected expenses arise. Staying flexible and open to revisiting the terms of support is vital for maintaining fairness and adequacy of support over time.

In navigating the child support and alimony landscape, the path is marked by a series of steps that demand both knowledge and negotiation. From understanding your legal entitlements and negotiating fair arrangements to enforcing payments and adjusting to new financial realities, each phase is critical in ensuring that the financial outcomes support the well-being and stability of the family. Through careful planning, informed negotiation, and a commitment to fairness, it's possible to navigate these challenges successfully, laying the groundwork for a stable and prosperous future.

6.4 UNDERSTANDING YOUR LEGAL RIGHTS IN CO-PARENTING

Navigating the landscape of co-parenting necessitates a clear understanding of the legal framework that defines the rights and responsibilities of each parent. This knowledge not only empowers you to make informed decisions but also ensures that the best interests of your children are always at the forefront.

Legal Rights and Responsibilities

In any co-parenting arrangement, both parents are vested with certain rights, but are also bound by responsibilities towards their children. These rights typically include the ability to make decisions regarding the child's education, healthcare, and religious upbringing. I once met a parent whose narcissistic ex told their son's school not to allow the parent to pick up their child, despite both parents having equal legal rights to do so. This attempt to exert control was not only manipulative, but also illegal under UK law, where both parents with parental responsibility have the right to be involved in their child's care unless a court orders otherwise.

Responsibilities, on the other hand, encompass providing financial support, ensuring the child's safety and well-being, and maintaining a supportive environment for the child's growth and development. It's crucial to familiarize yourself with these aspects, as they form the bedrock of co-parenting dynamics. Local family law clinics often provide workshops or consultations to help you understand these legal frameworks in the context of your specific situation.

Custody and Visitation

The terms of custody and visitation are often the most complex and emotionally charged aspects of co-parenting arrangements. Custody can be classified into physical custody, determining where the child lives, and legal custody, pertaining to who makes significant decisions about the child's life. Visitation rights, meanwhile, outline the non-custodial parent's access to the child. Crafting these agreements demands a delicate balance, focusing squarely on what serves the child's best interests. It's advisable to work with a mediator or family law specialist who can guide the negotiation process, ensuring that the final agreement reflects the needs of the child while respecting the rights of both parents.

Protective Orders and Safety

In situations where abuse or harassment is a concern, securing the safety of both the child and the custodial parent becomes paramount. Protective orders, also known as restraining orders, can be sought to prevent the abusive parent from coming into contact with the child or the co-parent. The process for obtaining a protective order varies by jurisdiction but generally involves filing a petition with the court, and providing evidence of abuse or harassment. It's vital to have all documentation in order, including any police reports, messages, or witness statements that corroborate the claim. Local domestic violence shelters and legal aid organizations can offer support and guidance through this process, ensuring you're not navigating these turbulent waters alone.

- **Safety Plan Template:** Crafting a comprehensive safety plan, with steps to take in case of emergencies, can provide peace of mind. This template should include emergency contacts, safe places, and legal resource information.

Accessing Legal Resources

The path to understanding and asserting your legal rights in co-parenting doesn't have to be walked alone. Numerous resources are available to offer guidance, support, and representation. Legal aid societies often provide free or low-cost legal services to those in need, focusing on family law issues including custody, visitation, and protective orders. Additionally, many online platforms offer directories of family law attorneys specializing in co-parenting and high-conflict scenarios. Taking advantage of these resources can equip you with the legal knowledge and support necessary to navigate co-parenting arrangements effectively.

Here's a comprehensive resource list to help you find legal aid, family law attorneys, and specialized support services for navigating co-parenting and custody challenges effectively.

Resource List for Legal Aid in Family Law

1. Legal Aid Organizations

- **Legal Services Corporation (LSC):** A federally funded non-profit organization that provides grants to local legal aid organizations across the U.S. Visit their website to find a legal aid provider in your state.
    - Website: LSC Website
- **American Bar Association (ABA) – Free Legal Answers**: This platform offers free legal advice on family law topics.

Users can submit questions to be answered by volunteer attorneys in their state.
- Website: ABA Free Legal Answers
- **LawHelp.org**: A comprehensive resource offering free legal aid referrals and information on family law issues such as custody, visitation, and domestic violence protection.
  - Website: LawHelp.org

2. Family Law Attorney Directories

- **Justia Lawyers Directory**: Search for family law attorneys by state and specialty, including those focused on co-parenting and high-conflict cases.
  - Website: Justia Lawyer Directory
- **FindLaw's Lawyer Directory**: A popular legal directory with a dedicated section for family law. Includes attorney profiles with specialties in custody and co-parenting arrangements.
  - Website: FindLaw Lawyer Directory
- **Avvo**: A legal advice and attorney directory platform where you can ask family law questions or search for specialized lawyers in your area.
  - Website: Avvo

3. Specialized Family Law Support

- **National Domestic Violence Hotline**: Provides support and resources for those experiencing high-conflict or abusive co-parenting situations. They offer confidential, free support via phone or chat.
  - Hotline: 1-800-799-SAFE (7233)
  - Website: thehotline.org

- **Parents' Rights Organizations**: Some non-profit organizations advocate for parental rights, offering legal resources and referrals to parents in custody battles. Examples include the **National Parents Organization** and **Divorce and Fathers Rights**.
    - National Parents Organization: Parents Organization Website
- **Online Legal Consultation Platforms**: Websites like **Rocket Lawyer** and **LegalZoom** provide affordable legal consultations and document preparation for family law cases. They offer easy access to professional advice and document templates.
    - Rocket Lawyer: Rocket Lawyer
    - LegalZoom: LegalZoom

4. State and Local Resources

- **Your Local Court's Family Law Self-Help Center**: Many courts have self-help centers or online resources with information about custody, visitation, and child support. Check your local court's website for resources.
- **State Bar Association**: Most state bar associations have family law resources and referral services for locating family law attorneys.

Understanding your legal rights and responsibilities, navigating custody and visitation agreements, ensuring safety through protective orders, and accessing legal resources form the pillars of legal preparedness in co-parenting. This framework not only supports your efforts to create a stable, nurturing environment for your children, but also empowers you to advocate for their best interests every step of the way.

6.5 PREPARING FOR LEGAL BATTLES: DOCUMENTATION AND EVIDENCE

In the realm of co-parenting with a narcissist, equipping yourself for potential legal disputes is akin to a gardener preparing the soil before planting. The groundwork of gathering, organizing, and presenting documentation and evidence is critical. This meticulous preparation not only strengthens your position, but also illuminates the truth of your circumstances, laying a solid foundation for your case.

The Importance of Documentation

Creating a thorough record of all interactions, decisions, and incidents related to your narcissistic ex is more than an administrative task, it's an essential strategy for safeguarding your rights and those of your children. Each email, text message, financial statement, and parenting plan agreement forms part of a narrative that can significantly influence legal outcomes. Start by setting up a dedicated filing system, whether digital or physical, to systematically categorize and store all relevant documents. This system becomes your repository of truth, a source you can draw from to substantiate your claims and counter any false narratives.

Maintaining a Detailed Log

Beyond formal documentation, keeping a detailed log of day-to-day interactions and notable incidents provides a chronological account that can be invaluable. This log should include dates, times, locations, and descriptions of interactions or events, especially those that highlight your ex's narcissistic behaviors or their impact on your children. Think of this as keeping a diary that captures not just facts but the emotional and psychological toll, offering a holistic view of your situation.

- Regular entries help capture details that might otherwise fade over time, ensuring you have a comprehensive account to reference.
- This log can also include your reflections on these interactions, providing insight into their effects on your well-being and that of your children.

Gathering Corroborative Evidence

While your documentation and log offer a solid starting point, bolstering your case with additional forms of evidence can be a game-changer. This might involve:

- Collecting witness statements from individuals who have observed the dynamics between you, your ex, and your children. These can provide third-party perspectives that validate your account.
- Seeking professional evaluations, such as from therapists or child psychologists, who can attest to the psychological impact of your ex's behavior on your children. Their expert opinions can carry significant weight in legal proceedings.

Working with Legal Professionals

Aligning with legal professionals who understand the nuances of your situation is critical. They can guide you in not only preparing your case but also in strategizing the best approach to achieve a favorable outcome. This partnership involves:

- Transparently sharing all collected documentation and evidence, allowing your legal team to build a robust case.
- Collaborating to identify key points and strategies that will resonate in court, focusing on safeguarding the best interests of your children and your personal safety.
- Your legal team can also advise on additional evidence that might strengthen your position, ensuring no stone is left unturned in your preparation.

When co-parenting with a narcissistic ex, documentation, evidence, and legal strategy all come together to form a shield that protects your rights and those of your children. It's a process that demands diligence, organization, and strategic thinking, but one that is crucial in navigating the complexities of legal disputes. This preparation not only fortifies your position, but also empowers you with the clarity and confidence needed to advocate effectively for your family's well-being.

As we conclude this exploration of preparing for legal battles, we are reminded of the power of documentation, detailed logs, corroborative evidence, and the strategic partnership with legal professionals. These elements collectively form a comprehensive approach to facing legal challenges, ensuring you are well-prepared and supported. Moving forward, the insights and strategies outlined here serve as a beacon, guiding you through the often daunting legal landscape and towards a resolution that honors the best interests of your children and your pursuit of peace and stability.

7

REDEFINING AND REBUILDING

I magine standing in front of a canvas, paintbrush in hand, with the entire spectrum of colors at your disposal. This isn't just any painting session, it's the first stroke on a blank canvas after years of following someone else's outline. This is what it feels like to rediscover and redefine your identity after a divorce, especially one involving the complex dynamics of co-parenting with a narcissistic ex. You're not just picking up where you left off; you're starting anew, with every color representing a different aspect of who you are and who you want to be.

7.1 REDEFINING YOUR IDENTITY AFTER DIVORCE

The Process of Self-Discovery

Rediscovering yourself outside of the confines of your marriage is not about reverting to the person you were before. It's about acknowledging the growth and changes that have taken place. Start by exploring interests that you might have set aside, or never even discovered. This could mean signing up for that pottery class you always found intriguing, or finally taking those guitar lessons. Through these activities, you're not just filling your time, you're peeling back layers to reveal new facets of your identity.

Here's a fun quiz designed to help you uncover hidden interests and hobbies that may spark joy and self-discovery. Whether you're looking to reconnect with passions you've put aside or try something entirely new, this quiz will guide you toward activities that align with the person you are now.

Quiz: Discover Your Hidden Interests

1. What kind of activities make you lose track of time?

   a. Reading or watching documentaries
   b. Creating art, crafts, or DIY projects
   c. Playing sports or being active outdoors

d. Learning new skills or hobbies online
   e. Socializing or joining group activities

2. Which of these topics are you most drawn to?

   a. History and culture
   b. Creative arts and design
   c. Health, fitness, and wellness
   d. Science, technology, or languages
   e. Community service or social causes

3. How do you feel about physical activities?

   a. Not my thing; I prefer calm activities.
   b. I enjoy creating things rather than being physical.
   c. I love them; physical activity helps me recharge.
   d. I enjoy some balance between mental and physical.
   e. I prefer activities that involve others or teams.

4. Which environment makes you feel the most inspired?

   a. A cozy corner with books and music
   b. An art studio or craft workshop
   c. Outdoors—nature, parks, beaches
   d. A classroom, museum, or lab
   e. A lively space with people and discussions

5. If you had a free afternoon, you'd most likely...

   a. Relax with a book, movie, or series
   b. Start a new project or try a creative hobby
   c. Go for a hike, run, or gym workout
   d. Learn something new or join a workshop

e. Volunteer, organize, or meet up with friends

6. How do you prefer to engage with your interests?

a. Solo, introspective, and peaceful activities
b. Expressive, hands-on, and personal projects
c. Physical, high-energy activities
d. Structured, educational, or skill-based activities
e. Collaborative, group, or social activities

Results

- **Mostly A's: Lover of Knowledge and Solitude**
    - Consider activities like joining a book club, taking a creative writing course, or exploring photography. These hobbies allow for quiet introspection while engaging your love for learning.
- **Mostly B's: Creative Maker**
    - Try art classes (pottery, painting), or crafting workshops. You enjoy hands-on activities that bring your creativity to life, making art and design ideal avenues for self-expression.
- **Mostly C's: Active Adventurer**
    - Outdoor hobbies like hiking, cycling, or even dance classes might be perfect for you. These activities not only keep you active but allow you to recharge through movement.
- **Mostly D's: Curious Learner**
    - Dive into classes, workshops, or online courses for skills like coding, cooking, or language learning. You thrive on structured learning and will enjoy hobbies that expand your knowledge base.

- **Mostly E's: Community Connector**
    - You're social and enjoy group-based activities. Consider joining local volunteer programs, community sports leagues, or a club to meet new people and give back to the community.

Overcoming Identity Loss

Feeling adrift is common as you grapple with who you are beyond your former role as a spouse. It's like looking in the mirror and not recognizing the person staring back. To combat this, set small, achievable goals for yourself that are entirely unrelated to your former partner or your role as a parent. Successfully achieving these goals, whether it's running a 5k or learning to cook a new dish, can bolster your self-esteem and help you regain a sense of individuality.

Reflection: Reclaiming Your Identity

Use the following journal prompts to explore and process feelings of identity loss. These prompts are designed to help you articulate your emotions, set goals, and track your progress as you rebuild a sense of self.

1. **Describe Your Current Feelings About Identity Loss**
    - How does it feel to look at yourself outside of the roles you once held? Write freely about any emotions, fears, or hopes that arise.

    _____

    _____

    _____

2. **Who Am I Beyond My Past Roles?**
    - List aspects of yourself that have nothing to do with your former role as a spouse or parent. Include qualities, dreams, or interests you may have set aside. Reflect on why each of these is important to you.

    _____

    _____

    _____

3. **Setting Small, Personal Goals**
    - Write down a few small goals you'd like to achieve on your own. These can be anything from trying a new activity, visiting a place you've always wanted to see, or learning a skill. How do you imagine reaching these goals will make you feel?

    _____

    _____

    _____

4. **Celebrate Small Wins**
    - Each time you accomplish one of your goals, return to this prompt. Describe what you achieved, how it made you feel, and any new insights you gained about yourself.

    _____
    _____
    _____

5. **Recognizing Your Progress**
    - Reflect on the past few weeks or months. How have your feelings about your identity changed since you started this journey? What growth do you see in yourself, and what challenges have you overcome?

    _____
    _____
    _____

6. **Embracing New Aspects of Self**
    - List any new interests, activities, or relationships that are now part of your life. How do they contribute to your evolving sense of self?

    _____
    _____
    _____

Remember, reclaiming your identity is a journey with ups and downs. Revisiting these prompts over time can help you see how far you've come and remind you of the strength you possess in creating a life that feels true to you.

Embracing New Roles

Your life post-divorce involves more than just adjusting to being single; it includes navigating the world as a co-parent and an individual with newfound independence. Embrace these roles by seeking out communities, both online and in-person, of people in similar situations. Sharing experiences and advice can not only provide support but also help redefine your understanding of what it means to be a successful, independent individual and parent.

Personal Growth and Development

Every challenge presents an opportunity for growth. The end of your marriage, while difficult, opens the door to personal development that might have been unimaginable within the relationship. Consider this time as a chance to enhance your skills or education, potentially leading to career advancement or a change in direction. Furthering your education, whether through formal degrees, online courses, or workshops, not only enriches your life but also sets a powerful example for your children about the value of lifelong learning and resilience.

Resource List for Free or Low-Cost Online Learning

1. Coursera

- Offers courses from top universities and companies, covering topics in business, technology, personal

development, and more. Many courses are free to audit, with an option to pay for certification.
- Website: Coursera

2. edX

- Provides access to high-quality courses from universities like Harvard, MIT, and Berkeley. Courses range from beginner to advanced levels and cover diverse subjects.
- Website: edX

3. Udemy

- Known for its wide variety of affordable courses, Udemy offers everything from coding and design to wellness and communication. Frequent sales make courses highly accessible.
- Website: Udemy

4. Khan Academy

- A free resource offering a broad range of subjects, especially in math, science, and humanities. Great for foundational knowledge and lifelong learning.
- Website: Khan Academy

5. LinkedIn Learning

- Offers courses focusing on professional skills, career development, and personal growth. Subscriptions include access to an extensive course library, with a free trial available.
- Website: LinkedIn Learning

6. FutureLearn

- Collaborates with universities and organizations worldwide to offer short courses in areas like psychology, business, and history. Many courses are free to join.
- Website: FutureLearn

7. Skillshare

- A subscription-based platform with courses on creative skills (e.g., design, writing) as well as entrepreneurship, marketing, and self-care. A free trial is available.
- Website: Skillshare

8. Alison

- Provides free online courses with options for certification in various fields such as IT, health, business, and personal development.
- Website: Alison

9. Harvard Online Learning

- Offers free and paid courses across subjects, including business, arts, health, and education. Some courses grant certificates upon completion.
- Website: Harvard Online Learning

10. Google Digital Garage

- Focuses on skills in digital marketing, data, and tech, with many courses free and some offering certification. Great for career advancement and business skills.

- Website: Google Digital Garage

In redefining your identity post-divorce, you're not erasing the past but building on it. It's about taking the experiences, lessons, and challenges you've faced and using them as a foundation for the new life you're creating. With each new interest explored, goal achieved, and role embraced, you paint another stroke on your canvas, gradually revealing a picture of who you are becoming—a vibrant, multifaceted individual with a life rich in color and possibility.

7.2 SETTING GOALS FOR A NEW BEGINNING

In the aftermath of divorce, especially from a narcissistic partner, the canvas of your life might feel dauntingly expansive. Yet, it's within this space that you have the unparalleled opportunity to paint a new, fulfilling picture of your future. Crafting this masterpiece involves not only vision but also strategic planning and a celebration of every stroke of progress, no matter how seemingly small.

Vision for the Future

Imagine sculpting a piece of art without a vision; the result would likely be unfocused and unsatisfying. Similarly, creating a future that resonates with your deepest desires starts with developing a clear, vivid picture of what you want. This vision acts as a guiding star, illuminating the path forward. Begin by asking yourself what brings you joy, fulfillment, and a sense of purpose. Visualize your ideal day, from the moment you wake until you retire at night. What activities fill your time? Who are the people around you? What accomplishments are you most proud of?

- **Visual Element:** A vision board can bring your aspirations to life. Collect images, quotes, and symbols that resonate with your goals and arrange them in a visual representation. This board serves as a daily reminder of where you're headed.

Goal-Setting Strategies

With your vision as the backdrop, it's time to map out the journey. Effective goal setting acts as the compass that directs your actions towards making this vision a reality. The SMART criteria—Specific, Measurable, Achievable, Relevant, and Time-bound—provide a solid framework for constructing your goals. For instance, rather than a vague aspiration like "I want to be happy," a SMART goal would be "I will dedicate one hour each week to pursuing my interest in painting, aiming to complete one piece per month."

- **Textual Element:** Break down larger goals into smaller, actionable steps. This segmentation transforms an overwhelming objective into manageable tasks, making progress more attainable.

Overcoming Obstacles

No path is without its hurdles, and the road to achieving your goals is no exception. Anticipating potential barriers allows you to prepare strategies for navigating them. For example, if time constraints pose a challenge to pursuing an interest, consider where in your schedule you can carve out moments for this passion. If fear of failure holds you back, remind yourself that every attempt, successful or not, is a learning opportunity and a step forward.

- **Interactive Element:** Reflect on past challenges you've overcome and the strategies that helped you succeed. This reflection can be a powerful source of motivation and insight when facing new obstacles.

Celebrating Progress

Acknowledging every step forward, no matter the size, is vital. This recognition fuels motivation and reinforces the value of your efforts. Did you stick to your plan of dedicating time to your personal interests this week? Celebrate it. Have you made strides in your career goals, perhaps by enrolling in a course or reaching out for mentorship? Acknowledge the progress. These celebrations can be as simple as a moment of gratitude or a small reward for yourself.

- **Textual Element:** Keep a progress journal where you note achievements related to your goals. Reviewing this journal offers tangible evidence of how far you've come, serving as encouragement to keep pushing forward.

In reimagining your life post-divorce, setting a vision for your future, employing strategic goal-setting, preparing for obstacles, and celebrating each step forward are instrumental. They transform the vast, blank canvas before you into a work of art that reflects your growth, resilience, and aspirations. As you navigate this process, remember that each brushstroke, no matter how insignificant it might seem, contributes to the beauty of the overall picture.

7.3 THE JOURNEY OF FINDING HAPPINESS AGAIN

Happiness, often seen as an elusive concept, takes on a new meaning post-divorce. It's no longer about grand gestures or monumental achievements; it's found in the simplicity of everyday moments and the peace that comes from within. This section explores the path to rediscovering joy and gratitude, crafting a life filled with purpose and letting go of the shadows of the past to welcome a brighter future.

Defining Happiness

Happiness post-divorce might appear different to the conventional portrayal we're accustomed to. It's crucial to pause and reflect on what genuinely brings you joy. For some, it might be the quiet moments alone with a book in hand, for others, the laughter-filled afternoons spent with children or friends. Acknowledging that happiness can be as diverse as the individuals experiencing it.

- Reflect on activities that have historically brought you joy or new interests you're curious about.
- Write down these reflections, noting how engaging in these activities affects your mood and outlook.
- Try different things - remember that if you try a new hobby and it isn't for you, change it! Taking the leap and putting yourself out there in new situations will allow you to grow and flourish.

Cultivating Joy and Gratitude

Incorporating practices that bring joy and gratitude into your daily routine can significantly impact your overall happiness. Simple acts of mindfulness, such as savoring your morning coffee or taking a few minutes to breathe deeply and appreciate the sunlight streaming through your window, can amplify feelings of joy. Gratitude, on the other hand, shifts the focus from what's missing to what's present in your life.

- Maintain a gratitude journal, listing three things you're thankful for each day. This practice can transform your perspective, highlighting the abundance of joy in your life.
- Engage in "joy spotting" during your day – actively looking for moments or things that bring a smile to your face.

Building a Fulfilling Life

Post-divorce life offers a blank slate, an opportunity to build a life that resonates with your deepest values and aspirations. This process begins with understanding what fulfillment means to you. Does it involve giving back to the community? Pursuing passions that were on hold? Or maybe it's about forging deeper connections with those around you.

- Identify areas of your life where you seek more fulfillment, whether in your career, personal growth, or relationships.
- Set actionable steps towards these goals, such as volunteering, enrolling in a class, or initiating regular meet-ups with friends.

Letting Go of the Past

Perhaps the most challenging yet liberating aspect of finding happiness again is releasing the hold of the past. Holding onto grievances or what-ifs only serves to cloud your present and future with bitterness and regret. Instead, focus on acceptance and forgiveness, not necessarily for the sake of others, but for your own peace of mind.

- Practice mindfulness or meditation to center yourself in the present, reducing the mental chatter about past events.
- Write a letter to your past self or your ex-partner, expressing all your unspoken thoughts and feelings. You don't have to send it; the act of writing can be a powerful tool for release and moving forward.

In redefining happiness post-divorce, you're not just searching for fleeting moments of joy but laying the foundation for a life rich in contentment and purpose. By pinpointing what happiness means to you, embracing daily practices of joy and gratitude, actively building a fulfilling life, and gently releasing the past, you open yourself to the myriad possibilities that lie ahead. This process isn't about erasing the challenges you've faced but about weaving them into the vibrant tapestry of your life, each thread contributing to the unique and beautiful picture of happiness you're creating.

7.4 DATING AFTER DIVORCE: WHEN AND HOW

Ready to Date Again

Deciding to explore romantic interests after a divorce is not a decision that comes lightly, especially when the echoes of a past relationship still linger. The question of "Am I ready?" is not just about having moved past your previous partner but about feeling emotionally stable and self-assured enough to share your life with someone new. To gauge readiness, consider whether the idea of dating excites you more than it makes you anxious. If memories of your ex don't invade your thoughts daily and you're pursuing interests and hobbies for your joy, these are positive signs. It can also be helpful to have a solid routine for managing co-parenting responsibilities, ensuring that new dynamics don't disrupt your children's equilibrium.

- **Reflective Exercise:** Write down what you envision for a future relationship. If your thoughts center more on what you hope to offer rather than what you seek to escape from, it's a hint that you might be ready to welcome someone new into your life.

Setting Healthy Expectations

When entering the dating scene again, it's crucial to set expectations that are both hopeful and grounded. Understand that everyone you meet carries their unique past and set of challenges. Looking for someone who understands the complexities of dating a single parent, especially one navigating co-parenting with a narcissistic ex, is important. Acknowledge that relationships develop at their own pace; instant connections are rare, and slow builds can be incredibly rewarding.

- Points for Consideration:
    - Accept that not every date will lead to a deeper connection, and that's okay.
    - Be honest about your situation and what you're looking for in a partner.
    - Recognize the value in learning about yourself through interactions with others, regardless of the outcome.

Navigating Dating Challenges

Dating as a single parent entails a balancing act between your needs and those of your children. When one parent is narcissistic, this balance becomes even more delicate. Before introducing a new partner to your children, be sure that the relationship is stable and likely to be a lasting one. Communicate openly with your children about the introduction, reassuring them of their paramount importance in your life. It's also wise to prepare for any backlash from your narcissistic ex, having strategies in place to manage attempts at interference or manipulation.

- Strategies for Smooth Transitions:
    - Discuss with your new partner the dynamics of co-parenting with a narcissistic ex, setting clear expectations for the role they will play.
    - Consider introducing your new partner to your children in neutral, low-pressure environments.
    - Ensure open lines of communication with your children, allowing them to express their feelings about the new relationship.

Protecting Your Well-Being

While the prospect of new love is exciting, your emotional well-being is paramount. It's essential to recognize red flags in potential partners, particularly behaviors reminiscent of your narcissistic ex. Trust your instincts; if something feels off, it likely is. Allow yourself the freedom to step back from dating if it becomes overwhelming. Remember, there's no timeline you need to adhere to, and taking time to ensure your happiness and health is crucial.

- Mindful Practices for Self-Preservation:
    - Keep a journal documenting your feelings about dating, identifying patterns or concerns that arise.
    - Develop a support network of friends or family members who can offer perspective and encouragement.
    - Engage in activities that promote your well-being and provide a break from the dating scene, such as meditation, exercise, or spending time in nature.

In this new chapter of your life, dating after divorce presents an opportunity for growth, joy, and the chance to share your journey with someone special. By approaching this experience with a sense of readiness, realistic expectations, careful navigation, and a commitment to your well-being, you open the door to fulfilling connections and the possibility of love that respects the complexities of your unique situation.

7.5 CRAFTING A POSITIVE LEGACY FOR YOUR CHILDREN

In the wake of a divorce, particularly one entangled with the complexities of a narcissistic relationship, the imprints we leave on our children's hearts and minds become more crucial than ever. It's here, amidst the upheaval, that we have a unique opportunity to lay down a legacy of resilience, values, and unconditional love—a beacon that can guide them through life's storms and into their sunshine.

Modeling Resilience

Life doesn't always unfold as planned, and it's through our responses to these unexpected turns that our children learn to navigate their own challenges. By facing obstacles head-on, with a blend of determination and flexibility, we demonstrate resilience in action. Whether it's a setback at work or a personal disappointment, discussing these experiences openly with our children, without dwelling on the negative, teaches them that setbacks are not endpoints but part of the growth process.

- Show them that asking for help is a strength, not a weakness, by reaching out for support when needed and then sharing how that support helped you overcome a challenge.
- Celebrate small victories together, reinforcing the message that progress, no matter how incremental, is valuable.

Help your children to overcome disappointment. My friend's daughter, who is 4-years-old, spent the whole week looking forward to seeing her mom (the narcissistic ex). Unfortunately, when the day came for them to spend time together the mom had an excuse and the plans fell through. The daughter was incredibly upset and disappointed, so my friend took this time to explain to her that things in life don't always go to plan and that it is often out of our control.

Teaching Values and Strengths

The values we instill in our children form the compass by which they navigate their lives. Honesty, empathy, respect—these are not just words but principles to live by. Engage in discussions about why these values matter, using stories from your life or books that illustrate these principles in action. Encourage them to share their thoughts and feelings, fostering an environment where open dialogue flourishes.

- Initiate family projects that reflect your values, like volunteering for community service, which can reinforce the importance of giving back and empathy.
- When they exhibit these values, acknowledge it. This recognition reinforces their internal motivation to act according to these principles.

Creating a Supportive Family Environment

The warmth of a loving home provides the security our children need to explore, take risks, and grow. This environment is built on consistency, understanding, and unconditional love. Strive to make your home a place where laughter is abundant, and every family member feels valued and heard.

- Establish rituals that bring the family together, such as family meal times, weekly game nights, or evening walks, creating shared moments that encourage closeness and communication.
- Encourage each family member to express their needs and thoughts, ensuring everyone has a voice in family decisions and activities.

Leaving a Legacy of Love and Strength

The most enduring legacy we can leave our children is the knowledge that they are loved unconditionally and possess the inner strength to face whatever life throws their way. This legacy is built day by day, through our actions, our words, and the lessons we share. It's about showing them, through our own lives, that love is not diminished by distance or circumstance and that strength is not about never falling but about having the courage to rise again.

- Write letters to your children on special occasions, sharing your hopes and dreams for them, your pride in their accomplishments, and your commitment to supporting them always. These letters can become cherished reminders of your love and belief in their strength.
- Foster a spirit of independence, encouraging them to pursue their passions and make their own decisions, while also making it clear that your support and love are unwavering.

In laying down these foundations for our children, we give them more than just lessons for the present - we equip them with the tools they need to build their futures. It's in the resilience they see modeled before them, the values they carry in their hearts, the warmth of their home environment, and the knowledge of their inherent strength and worth, that they find the guidance and support to forge their paths in life.

As we move forward, let's remember that our efforts today are not just about navigating the aftermath of a divorce or the challenges of co-parenting. They're about sowing seeds for a future where our children thrive, grounded in love, resilience, and the strength of their character. This is the legacy we strive to leave—a legacy that, brick by brick, builds a stronger, more compassionate world.

8

HIGH-STAKES CO-PARENTING

Picture a tightrope walker, making their way across a slender wire suspended high above the ground. Every step is measured, every breath calculated to maintain balance and ensure safety. This image mirrors the delicate act of co-parenting with a narcissistic ex, especially when tensions escalate. It's about finding equilibrium in a situation that constantly threatens to throw you off balance.

8.1 NAVIGATING SMEAR CAMPAIGNS AND PUBLIC PERCEPTION

In the aftermath of a relationship with a narcissistic partner, especially when children are involved, the challenges you face may not always be confined to the privacy of personal interactions. Sometimes, they spill over into the public domain, manifesting as smear campaigns designed to tarnish your reputation and isolate you from your community. Understanding how to navigate these treacherous waters, while maintaining your dignity and protecting your public image, requires a mix of strategic thinking and emotional resilience.

Smear campaigns typically involve the narcissistic ex-partner spreading false accusations, rumors, and exaggerated tales of your supposed misdeeds to friends, family, and sometimes even to public forums and social media. Recognizing these actions for what they are—a desperate attempt to control the narrative and undermine your credibility—is the first step in formulating your response.

Understanding Smear Campaigns

At the heart of a smear campaign is the narcissist's need to feel superior and in control. By discrediting you, they aim to shift any blame away from themselves, often playing the victim to garner sympathy and support from those around them. This tactic can be particularly damaging, leading to social isolation and emotional distress. Recognizing this pattern is crucial, as it allows you to see the campaign for what it is: a manipulation strategy, not a reflection of your character or parenting.

Maintaining Integrity

Your integrity is your shield against the onslaught of a smear campaign. Staying true to yourself and not succumbing to the temptation to retaliate in kind is vital. Here are a few strategies to consider:

- Stay calm and collected in public and private. Reacting emotionally or defensively can be seen as an admission of guilt.
- Keep your communications with the narcissist in writing, maintaining a record of your interactions that can speak to your character and parenting.
- Focus on the well-being of your children. Your actions and decisions should always come back to what is best for them, not what will "win" against the narcissist.

Legal Recourse

There are instances where a smear campaign crosses the line from hurtful gossip into the realm of defamation or harassment. In these cases, legal recourse may be necessary to protect your reputation and your peace of mind.

- Consult with a legal professional about the possibility of a defamation suit if false statements made by your ex have caused tangible damage to your reputation or livelihood.
- Consider a restraining order if the smear campaign includes threats to your safety or that of your children.

Remember, legal action is not about revenge but about setting clear boundaries and protecting your rights.

Support Networks

One of the narcissist's goals in launching a smear campaign is to isolate you. Counter this by leaning on and strengthening your support network. Friends, family, and professional support circles can offer not only emotional backing but also serve as a buffer against the lies being spread about you.

- Be open with your friends and family about what you're going through. While you don't need to share every detail, letting them know you're facing false accusations can help preempt any doubts sown by the narcissist.
- Engage with support groups, either in person or online, specifically for those navigating high-conflict co-parenting or recovering from relationships with narcissists. Here, you'll find understanding, practical advice, and perhaps most importantly, validation of your experiences.

Navigating the choppy waters of smear campaigns and managing public perception when co-parenting with a narcissistic ex requires a balanced approach that prioritizes your integrity, legal protections, and the cultivation of a strong support network. Remember, the aim is not to "win" against the smear campaign but to protect your well-being and ensure you and your children can move forward positively.

8.2 CRISIS MANAGEMENT: WHEN TO SEEK PROFESSIONAL HELP

In the maelstrom of high-conflict co-parenting, storms can brew suddenly, catching you off guard and threatening to capsize your carefully maintained balance. It's in these tempestuous moments that recognizing the need for professional intervention becomes a lifeline, not a sign of defeat. Understanding the warning signs, crafting an emergency plan, tapping into professional resources, and emphasizing self-care are crucial steps in navigating through the storm.

Recognizing a Crisis

A crisis can manifest in various ways, subtly creeping into your life or erupting suddenly. It might appear as a noticeable shift in your or your children's behavior, an uncharacteristic withdrawal from social activities, or an overwhelming sense of anxiety or depression that refuses to abate. Physical symptoms, such as insomnia or a persistent feeling of exhaustion, can also signal that the situation has escalated beyond your current coping mechanisms. Acknowledging these signs without judgment is the first step towards seeking the help you need.

Emergency Plans

Having a plan in place before a crisis hits can provide a sense of security and control in otherwise chaotic situations. Think of this plan as a life raft, meticulously prepared and ready to deploy:

- **Contacts List:** Compile a list of emergency contacts, including trusted friends, family members, and

professionals like your therapist or lawyer, who can provide immediate support.
- **Safety Measures:** Outline steps to ensure physical safety for you and your children, including safe places to stay if needed.
- **Crisis Hotlines:** Keep a list of crisis hotlines easily accessible. These can offer immediate assistance and guidance, acting as a beacon in the darkest moments.

Professional Resources

Finding the right professional help can feel like navigating a labyrinth, particularly when time is of the essence. Start by identifying therapists or counselors experienced in dealing with high-conflict family dynamics or the aftermath of narcissistic relationships. Many mental health professionals now offer online sessions, providing flexibility and access regardless of your location. In addition, legal professionals specializing in high-conflict co-parenting can offer crucial advice and intervention strategies to protect your rights and well-being.

- **Therapists and Counselors:** Look for professionals with specific experience in narcissistic abuse recovery and high-conflict co-parenting.
- **Crisis Hotlines:** Organizations such as the National Domestic Violence Hotline provide immediate support and advice.
- **Legal Assistance:** Connect with legal aid services or family law attorneys experienced in handling high-conflict cases, ensuring they're familiar with the intricacies of narcissistic behavior.

Self-Preservation

At the heart of crisis management lies the principle of self-preservation. It's about recognizing when the wisest course of action is to retreat and regroup rather than forge ahead. This might mean temporarily stepping back from contentious interactions with your ex, focusing on stabilizing your emotional state, or even making the difficult decision to involve law enforcement or seek a protective order in situations where safety is compromised. Remember, prioritizing your well-being and that of your children is not selfish—it's necessary.

In the journey of high-conflict co-parenting, encountering storms is inevitable. Yet, within these challenges lie opportunities for growth, resilience, and eventually, moments of calm. By staying attuned to the signs of a brewing crisis, preparing an emergency plan, seeking out the right professional support, and prioritizing your own well-being, you navigate these turbulent waters with strength and grace. This approach not only ensures your safety and stability but also models for your children the importance of self-care and seeking help when needed.

As we move forward, let's carry with us the understanding that crisis management is not just about weathering the storm—it's about emerging on the other side, ready to continue the journey with renewed resolve and resources at our disposal.

8.3 TECHNIQUES FOR EMOTIONAL DETACHMENT IN CONFLICT

In the dance of co-parenting with a narcissist, maintaining your emotional equilibrium is akin to remaining upright and poised, even when the floor beneath you shifts unexpectedly. This section explores strategies to maintain this balance, ensuring that you stay emotionally insulated even in the face of provocation.

Building Emotional Barriers

Imagine constructing a fortress around your emotions; not to isolate yourself, but to shield your inner peace from the arrows of conflict and manipulation. This fortress is built on the foundation of understanding your worth and recognizing that a narcissist's attempts to ruffle your emotions say more about their character than yours.

- **Personal Affirmations:** Start your day with affirmations that reinforce your self-esteem and worth. Simple statements like "I am in control of my emotions" or "I choose peace over conflict" can be powerful reminders.
- **Visualize a Barrier:** When faced with potential conflict, visualize an actual barrier—perhaps a wall or shield—between you and the narcissist. This mental image serves as a buffer, helping to deflect their words or actions.

Mindfulness Practices

Mindfulness is the anchor that keeps you grounded in the storm of co-parenting conflict. It involves being present in the moment and observing your thoughts and emotions without judgment. This awareness gives you the clarity to respond rather than react impulsively.

- **Breathing Exercises:** Utilize deep breathing exercises to center yourself in moments of stress. Inhale deeply, hold for a moment, and exhale slowly, focusing solely on the rhythm of your breath.

- **Mindful Observation:** Practice observing your surroundings with detailed attention for a few minutes each day. This practice trains your mind to focus on the present, reducing the impact of external stressors.

Self-Soothing Strategies

Self-soothing is the art of calming your mind and body, restoring a sense of tranquility amid turmoil. It's about having a set of personal tools ready to deploy when you feel your emotional balance wavering.

- **Create a Calm Playlist:** Music has a profound effect on our emotions. Compile a playlist of songs that bring you peace or joy. Turn to this playlist when you need to uplift your mood or calm your nerves.
- **Physical Comfort:** Identify physical activities that provide comfort. This could be a warm bath, a brisk walk, or a series of gentle stretches. These activities offer a double benefit: they distract you from stress and engage your body in positive movement.

Selective Engagement

Choosing when and how to engage with a narcissistic ex is perhaps the most strategic decision you can make. It's about picking battles wisely, ensuring that you only invest your energy in matters truly worth your time and emotional effort.

- **Criteria for Engagement:** Establish clear criteria for what necessitates engagement. If an issue directly impacts your children's well-being or safety, it likely meets these criteria. If it's a matter that doesn't have a

substantial impact or is designed to provoke, consider stepping back.
- **Time Limits:** Set strict time limits for any necessary interactions. This could mean limiting phone calls to a specific duration or setting a timer when drafting responses to emails or texts.
- **Neutral Ground:** Whenever possible, choose neutral settings for in-person interactions, such as public places. These environments can subtly influence a more civil demeanor from both parties.

By implementing these strategies, you fortify your emotional resilience, ensuring that you navigate co-parenting conflicts with a sense of calm and detachment. This approach doesn't just protect your well-being; it also models healthy coping mechanisms for your children, teaching them valuable lessons in managing their emotions and interactions.

9

STEPPING INTO YOUR POWER

Imagine you're standing at the edge of a cliff, overlooking a vast ocean. The waves crash against the rocks in a symphony of nature's resilience and power. Now picture yourself, not as an onlooker, but as part of this scene—poised to dive into the waters below, ready to swim with purpose and strength. This moment encapsulates the essence of personal empowerment: a blend of courage, determination, and the readiness to plunge into the depths of your potential.

In the context of co-parenting with a narcissistic ex, empowerment isn't just a lofty ideal, it's your lifeline. It's about reclaiming your voice, setting boundaries that protect your peace, and navigating the challenges with confidence. Let's explore how you can build a personal empowerment plan that anchors you, allowing you to swim through the turbulent waters with resilience and grace.

9.1 BUILDING A PERSONAL EMPOWERMENT PLAN

Setting Empowerment Goals

Goals are the compass that guides your empowerment journey. They should be specific, like deciding to learn a new skill that boosts your independence, or broad, such as aspiring to achieve a sense of peace and stability in your co-parenting arrangement. The key is to ensure these goals resonate with your vision of empowerment.

- Start by listing areas in your life where you feel disempowered. Is it in decision-making? Financial independence? Emotional well-being?
- For each area, set a goal that shifts the narrative. For example, if financial independence is a concern, a goal might be to create a budget or start a savings plan.

Skills and Knowledge Acquisition

Empowerment blooms from knowledge and skills. It's about arming yourself with the tools needed to navigate, not just the *legalities* of co-parenting with a narcissist, but also the *emotional* landscapes.

- Consider enrolling in workshops or seminars that focus on effective communication, legal rights, or financial planning.
- Online platforms offer a plethora of courses that fit various schedules and needs. A weekend workshop on negotiation skills, for instance, can transform how you interact with your ex.

Personal Advocacy

Advocating for yourself is a cornerstone of empowerment. It means speaking up for your needs, defending your boundaries, and seeking fair treatment in all aspects of your life.

- Practice scenarios where you might need to advocate for yourself. This could be in conversations with your ex, meetings with lawyers, or discussions with your children's teachers.
- Remember, advocacy is as much about listening and understanding as it is about speaking. It's a two-way street.

Celebrating Milestones

Every step forward deserves recognition. Celebrating milestones, no matter how small, reinforces your progress and bolsters your self-worth.

- Create a "victory log" where you record every success, be it successfully mediating a dispute with your ex, or a week where you stuck to your budget.
- Share these wins with friends or family who support your empowerment journey. Sometimes, external acknowledgment amplifies the sense of achievement.

Visual Element: Empowerment Plan Template

Imagine a chart, divided into four quadrants, each representing a key component of your empowerment plan: Goals, Skills, Advocacy, and Milestones. This visual template serves as a daily reminder of your empowerment journey, tracking progress and highlighting areas for growth.

- **Quadrant 1 (Goals):** List your empowerment goals, with checkboxes for milestones achieved.
- **Quadrant 2 (Skills):** Detail the skills and knowledge you aim to acquire, with space for course names, dates, and outcomes.
- **Quadrant 3 (Advocacy):** Keep notes on instances where you successfully advocated for yourself, including the scenario and outcome.
- **Quadrant 4 (Milestones):** Record the milestones you've reached, celebrating each with a brief description and date.

Interactive Element: Reflective Journaling Prompts

To deepen your empowerment journey, reflective journaling offers a space to explore your thoughts, emotions, and responses to the challenges faced. Here are some prompts to get you started:

- **Prompt 1:** "When I feel disempowered, the underlying fear or belief fueling this feeling is..."
- **Prompt 2:** "A situation where I successfully advocated for myself was... What I learned from this experience is..."
- **Prompt 3:** "One skill I want to develop to enhance my empowerment is... Because..."

Textual Element: Resource List for Self-Advocacy

A curated list of resources, including books, websites, and local organizations, can provide additional support and information on self-advocacy and empowerment:

- **Books:** Titles such as "Boundaries" by Dr. Henry Cloud and Dr. John Townsend offer insights into setting and maintaining healthy limits.
- **Websites:** Platforms like the National Domestic Violence Hotline offer advice and support for those navigating abusive or high-conflict co-parenting situations.
- **Local Organizations:** Listings of local support groups or workshops focusing on empowerment and self-advocacy, tailored to those exiting relationships with narcissists.

Empowerment in the context of co-parenting with a narcissist is an ongoing process, a steady accumulation of knowledge, skills, self-advocacy, and milestones celebrated. It's a journey marked by personal growth, resilience, and the reclamation of your voice and power. Through careful planning, continuous learning, and unwavering advocacy for your needs, you not only navigate the challenges but also emerge stronger, more confident, and truly empowered.

9.2 ADVOCATING FOR YOUR CHILDREN'S RIGHTS

In the complex dynamics of co-parenting with a narcissistic ex, our children's well-being remains our top priority. It requires us to become adept at advocating for their rights, ensuring they receive the support and care they deserve. This task encompasses a broad spectrum of activities, from understanding their rights to teaching them how to stand up for themselves in various settings.

Understanding Children's Rights

First and foremost, a deep dive into the rights of children within the legal and emotional framework of high-conflict co-parenting situations is crucial. Children have the right to a safe and stable environment, access to education, and the freedom to express their thoughts and feelings. They also have the right to maintain a healthy relationship with both parents, where possible. A mother I know would drive her two children three hours every fortnight to visit their father, a narcissistic ex who never made the effort himself. She prioritized her children's right to have a relationship with their father and went out of her way to ensure they had the opportunity to spend time with him, despite his lack of effort. Familiarizing yourself with these rights, as outlined in legal statutes and psychological best practices, equips you with the ability to defend and advocate for these essentials effectively.

- Review legal documents and literature on children's rights in your jurisdiction.
- Consult with child welfare professionals and legal advisors to understand the nuances of these rights in high-conflict scenarios.

School and Social Advocacy

Our children spend a significant portion of their time in school and social settings, places where the impact of a turbulent home life can manifest in various ways. Advocating for your child in these environments involves:

- Regular communication with teachers and school counselors, ensuring they are aware of the home situation without oversharing unnecessary details. This awareness can help them to provide additional support or understanding to your child.
- Encouraging extracurricular activities that bolster your child's confidence and provide a healthy outlet for stress.
- Attending PTA meetings and school events, staying engaged in your child's educational journey, and building a network of supportive adults around them.

Legal Advocacy for Children

Navigating the legal system to protect and advocate for your children's rights and best interests is sometimes necessary. This might involve seeking modifications to custody arrangements, advocating for the child's voice to be heard in legal decisions, or ensuring their emotional and physical needs are met through court orders.

- Prepare a clear, fact-based case for any legal action, documenting instances where your child's rights or well-being were compromised.
- Work closely with a family law attorney who understands the high-conflict nature of your co-parenting situation and is committed to prioritizing your child's best interests.

- Support your child through the legal process, explaining in age-appropriate terms what is happening and reassuring them of your unconditional support.

Empowering Your Children

One of the most enduring gifts we can give our children is the ability to advocate for themselves. This empowerment comes from teaching them to understand their own rights, to communicate their needs respectfully, and to stand up for themselves when necessary.

- Start conversations about feelings and rights in everyday contexts, encouraging your child to express themselves openly and honestly.
- Role-play scenarios where they might need to assert themselves, providing them with language and strategies to do so effectively.
- Celebrate instances where your child successfully uses these skills, reinforcing the importance of self-advocacy.

In the fabric of high-conflict co-parenting, weaving a strong thread of advocacy for our children's rights is not just an act of protection—it's an investment in their future resilience and independence. By teaching them to recognize and assert their own rights, we prepare them to navigate the world with confidence, knowing they have a strong advocate in their corner.

9.3 USING YOUR EXPERIENCE TO HELP OTHERS

From the ashes of hardship, a phoenix rises, not just to soar again, but to light the way for others still struggling in the darkness. This metaphor beautifully captures the transformation of personal pain into a mission of support and guidance for those embarking on a similar path of co-parenting with a narcissist. The scars of our experiences, rather than symbols of past battles, become marks of wisdom, empathy, and strength that we can offer to others.

Turning Pain into Purpose

The road walked through the storm of narcissistic co-parenting is fraught with unique challenges and lessons learned. Each obstacle overcome and each tear shed carves out a deeper well of understanding and compassion within us. This well becomes a source from which we can draw to quench the thirst of others navigating this difficult terrain.

- Reflect on the pivotal moments and insights gained from your experiences. What were the turning points? What wisdom can you distill from these?
- Consider writing a personal manifesto based on these reflections, a declaration of how you intend to use your journey to light the path for others.

Volunteering and Mentoring

Giving back through volunteering and mentoring offers both a direct impact on the mentees, and a therapeutic outlet for the mentor. Organizations dedicated to supporting individuals going through high-conflict separations or divorces often seek volunteers with firsthand experience to provide empathy, understanding, and practical advice.

- Reach out to local support groups, legal aid societies, or online communities to offer your time and insights. Many

are in dire need of volunteers who can relate personally to the struggles of their members.
- Engage in mentorship programmes, either formally through these organizations, or informally by connecting with individuals in your community. This one-to-one support can be invaluable to someone feeling isolated in their struggles.

Public Speaking and Writing

Sharing your story through public speaking and writing not only raises awareness, but also enables you to connect with others on a deeply personal level to offer them hope and practical strategies.

- Start a blog or contribute articles to existing platforms focused on divorce, co-parenting, or overcoming narcissistic abuse. Your written words can reach individuals worldwide and provide comfort and guidance.
- Offer to speak at events organized by support groups, schools, or community centers. Verbally sharing your story, including the challenges you faced, and the strategies that helped you cope, can inspire and empower others in similar situations.
- Use creativity as an outlet and write poems about your feelings and experiences. Attend open mic poetry nights to share your poetry with an audience.

Creating Resources

Developing resources such as guides, blogs, or workshops allows you to compile your learnings and advice together in accessible formats. These resources become tools others can use to navigate their journey more smoothly.

- Compile a guide based on the most effective strategies you employed in dealing with your narcissistic ex-partner. Include practical advice, from legal tips to emotional coping mechanisms.
- Launch a blog where you not only share your personal experiences but also invite contributions from others. This can become a vibrant community of support and exchange.
- Organize workshops, either in person or online, focusing on specific aspects of co-parenting with a narcissist, like setting boundaries, effective communication, or self-care. These workshops can provide a structured environment for learning and discussion.

In transforming personal pain into a purposeful mission, each step taken to support, guide, and uplift others not only contributes to their empowerment but also reinforces our own personal healing and growth. Through volunteering, mentoring, public speaking, writing, and creating resources, we extend a hand to those still in the throes of co-parenting with a narcissist, offering them the wisdom of our experiences and the assurance that they are not alone. This endeavor, while born from our struggles, blossoms into a powerful movement of shared strength and collective resilience, lighting the way for countless others on this challenging path.

9.4 ESTABLISHING A CO-PARENTING ADVOCACY GROUP

In the realm of navigating life post-divorce, especially when entangled with a narcissistic ex-partner, the power of community cannot be overstated. The creation of a co-parenting advocacy group serves as a beacon for those in similar situations, offering a space not just for support, but for collective action. Here's how you can lay the foundations for such a group to transform individual struggles into a unified force for change and empowerment.

Creating a Support Network

The initial step involves reaching out to others who share your experiences. This can be achieved through various platforms, such as social media groups, community center bulletin boards, or connections made during therapy sessions or participating in support groups. The goal is to gather a diverse group of individuals, each bringing their unique perspective and wisdom to the table.

- **Initial Meetup:** Organize a casual meeting, perhaps in a coffee shop or a quiet park, where everyone can introduce themselves and share their stories. This creates a sense of community and mutual understanding right from the start.
- **Regular Meetings:** Set up regular gatherings, whether weekly or monthly, to discuss challenges, celebrate victories, and simply offer each other a listening ear. These can rotate between in-person and virtual meetings to accommodate everyone.
- **Private Online Forum:** Create a private online forum or social media group where members can post updates, ask for advice, and share resources at any time. This ensures continuous support and accessibility for all members.

Sharing Resources and Strategies

With the network established, the next focus is on the exchange of invaluable resources and strategies that have proven beneficial in navigating the complexities of co-parenting with a narcissist. This includes legal advice, therapeutic techniques, financial planning tips, and effective communication strategies.

- **Guest Speakers:** Invite professionals such as family law attorneys, therapists, and financial advisors to share their expertise during meetings. This provides members with direct access to professional guidance and answers to their pressing questions. Note that you will likely need to pay for their time.
- **Resource Library:** Compile a digital or physical library of books, articles, and other materials related to co-parenting, narcissistic behavior, and personal empowerment. Make this library available to all group members.
- **Workshops:** Organize workshops that focus on developing specific skills, such as effective communication with a narcissistic ex, setting and maintaining boundaries, or managing stress and emotional well-being.

Community Awareness

Raising awareness about the challenges of co-parenting with a narcissist is crucial, not only for garnering broader support, but also for advocating for societal and legal changes that can benefit affected families. This involves engaging with the wider community and leveraging the group's collective voice.

- **Public Events:** Host public events, such as talks or panel discussions, where group members can share their experiences and insights with a broader audience. This can help break down stigmas and foster a greater understanding of the challenges faced.

- **Collaboration with Local Organizations:** Partner with local organizations that focus on family services, domestic abuse prevention, and legal aid to reach a wider audience and offer more comprehensive support.
- **Advocacy Campaigns:** Launch campaigns aimed at advocating for legal reforms that protect the rights and well-being of parents and children navigating high-conflict co-parenting situations. This could include petitions, awareness drives, and meetings with local representatives.

Empowerment through Unity

At the heart of the co-parenting advocacy group is the principle of empowerment through unity. By bringing together individuals who have faced the loneliness and challenges of co-parenting with a narcissistic ex, the group becomes more than just a support network, it transforms into a powerful agent of change.

- **Success Stories:** Encourage members to share their success stories, highlighting the strategies that helped them overcome specific challenges. These stories serve as a powerful testament to the strength and resilience of the group.
- **Mentorship Program:** Establish a mentorship program within the group, pairing newer members with those who have navigated the co-parenting path for a longer time. This one-on-one support can be incredibly beneficial to those just starting their journey.
- **Community Projects:** Engage in community projects that reflect the group's mission, such as supporting local shelters or organizing educational workshops for the public. These projects not only raise awareness but also

reinforce the group's role as a positive force in the community.

Through the establishment of a co-parenting advocacy group, individuals who once felt isolated in their struggles find a sense of belonging, support, and collective strength. This group becomes a conduit for sharing knowledge, advocating for change, and empowering each member to reclaim their voice and agency in the co-parenting journey. With each shared story, resource exchange, and community engagement, the group not only supports its members but also contributes to a broader understanding and empathy towards the complexities of co-parenting with a narcissistic ex, laying the groundwork for societal and legal advancements that can benefit countless families.

9.5 THE POWER OF STORYTELLING: SHARING YOUR JOURNEY

Sharing the highs and lows of navigating life tied to a narcissist opens a channel for healing that many might not initially recognize. This act, often viewed as a mere recount of past events, holds a transformative power for both the narrator and the audience. It's in the act of opening up, of laying bare the struggles and triumphs, that a shared bond of understanding and empathy is created. This connection transcends the individual, touching the lives of others in ways that are both profound and unexpected.

Healing Through Sharing

The act of storytelling isn't just about unburdening oneself or seeking a platform for one's voice. It's a therapeutic process that offers a sense of liberation from the emotional weight carried for so long. For the storyteller, it's a journey through their own narrative, viewing their experiences through a new lens and finding meaning in the chaos. For those on the receiving end, it's a mirror to their own experiences or a window into a world they've never known, fostering a deeper sense of empathy and understanding.

- Sharing your story in support groups can foster a sense of community and collective healing.
- Writing a personal account, whether in a journal or a blog, allows for reflection and catharsis.

Finding Your Voice

Every individual's story is as unique as their fingerprint, and finding the most authentic way to express it is crucial. Some may find solace and strength in writing, their words flowing freely in the quiet moments of reflection. Others may discover their voice in speaking, the spoken word offering a directness and immediacy that connects deeply with listeners. The medium matters less than the authenticity of the expression. It's about finding the channel that resonates most with you, where your true voice can emerge unfiltered and potent.

- Experiment with different mediums of storytelling to discover what feels most natural and empowering.
- Consider joining a writing workshop or a public speaking group to refine your skills and gain confidence in your voice.

Inspiring Change

The ripples created by sharing your story can extend far beyond the immediate circle of listeners or readers. They can spark change on a larger scale, challenging societal norms, influencing policy, and reshaping the narrative around co-parenting with a narcissist. When stories are shared, they can illuminate the dark corners of experience that many shy away from, pushing these conversations into the public sphere and advocating for a deeper understanding and better support systems.

- Collaborate with advocacy groups to use your story as part of broader campaigns for change.
- Engage with media outlets or social platforms to bring wider attention to the realities of co-parenting with a narcissist.

Building A Legacy Of Hope

In sharing your story, you're doing more than recounting past events; you're building a legacy. This legacy, constructed from your resilience and determination, stands as a beacon of hope for those still ensnared in their struggle. It says, "You are not alone, and there is a way forward." This legacy transcends the personal, becoming a collective narrative of strength, hope, and the indomitable human spirit. It's a testament to the power of sharing one's story, not just as a means of personal catharsis, but as a way to light the path for others.

- Share your story at conferences or seminars focused on family dynamics, legal challenges, or mental health, contributing to a broader discourse on overcoming adversity.
- Mentor someone who is navigating the early stages of co-parenting with a narcissist, offering your story as a roadmap for their journey.

As this chapter folds, remember the profound impact your narrative can have. From the intimate act of sharing comes healing, understanding, and the potential to inspire profound change. It's through these stories that we connect, find common ground, and forge a path forward, not just for ourselves, but for the community at large. As we move on, let's carry the lessons learned and the strength gained into every aspect of our lives, ready to face new challenges with resilience and hope.

EMPOWERING OTHERS ON THE JOURNEY

You've made it through *Co-Parenting with a Narcissistic Ex 101*, and I truly hope it's brought you insights, strength, and practical strategies to help you navigate this challenging path with confidence and calm.

Now, you have the opportunity to help others who are walking a similar road. By leaving an honest review on Amazon, you'll be guiding others toward the support and tools they need to protect their peace and focus on what matters most—their children.

Your review doesn't just share your perspective; it becomes part of a supportive community for others facing these struggles. Thank you for making a difference by sharing your experience.

With gratitude,

Casey Jordan

CONCLUSION

As we reach the culmination of our journey together, it's time to reflect on the path we've traversed. From the initial steps of understanding the intricate web of narcissism to the empowering strategies of communication, boundary-setting, and prioritizing our well-being, our expedition has been one of profound discovery and growth. Together, we've delved into recognizing narcissistic behaviors, mastering communication devoid of conflict, safeguarding our children from the fallout, and, most importantly, reclaiming our lives with a newfound resilience and hope.

The essence of our journey underscores the criticality of grasping the nature of narcissism, enabling us to predict and navigate the tumultuous behaviors that come with co-parenting under such dynamics. The Gray Rock Method and other communication strategies we've explored are not mere tactics, but lifelines that maintain our sanity and serenity amidst storms. The fortitude found in setting and enforcing boundaries, coupled with the delicate art of supporting our children through these trials, forms the backbone of our resilience. And let's not forget the solace and rejuvenation that comes from self-care and the pursuit of personal fulfillment post-divorce, which paves the way for our ultimate empowerment.

This book is not meant to be a transient companion but a perennial resource to guide you through the varying phases of co-parenting with a narcissist. I encourage you to revisit its chapters as you encounter new challenges and milestones. Let it be a beacon of support and wisdom as you maneuver through the complexities of this journey.

In the spirit of solidarity, I urge you to reach out and weave networks of support with those who tread similar paths. There's immeasurable strength in shared experiences and collective wisdom. These networks are not just support systems but lifelines that validate our struggles and victories.

Your story, too, holds power—the power to heal, inspire, and encourage. Sharing your narrative, be it in intimate support groups or the broader expanses of social media, can be both cathartic for you and illuminating for others. It reminds us that we're part of a larger community bound by shared challenges and triumphs.

Professional guidance, be it from legal advisors or mental health practitioners, remains an indispensable pillar of support. Their expertise can tailor strategies to our unique situations, offering clarity and direction when the way forward seems obscured.

Amidst the trials and tribulations, let us not overlook the importance of self-compassion. The journey is arduous, and it's natural to encounter moments of doubt and struggle. Remember, caring for yourself is paramount—not just for your well-being but for your capacity to nurture and protect your children.

As we part ways, I leave you with a message of hope—a beacon to light your path. Despite the adversities inherent in co-parenting with a narcissist, a brighter horizon lies ahead. With the right strategies, a supportive network, and unwavering resilience, you can navigate this journey successfully. You're not alone in this battle. Together, we can emerge from the shadows of narcissism into a life marked by happiness, fulfillment, and empowerment.

May you carry forward the lessons, strategies, and insights from our time together, using them as tools to carve out a path filled with light and promise. Here's to a future where you stand strong, empowered, and enveloped in the peace and happiness you so richly deserve.

REFERENCES

Narcissistic personality disorder - Symptoms and causes https://www.mayoclinic.org/diseases-conditions/narcissistic-personality-disorder/symptoms-causes/syc-20366662

How Narcissistic Parenting Can Affect Children https://www.psychologytoday.com/us/blog/the-legacy-of-distorted-love/201802/how-narcissistic-parenting-can-affect-children

What Is a Covert Narcissist? Understanding the Signs and ... https://apn.com/resources/what-is-a-covert-narcissist-understanding-the-signs-and-symptoms/#:

8 Ways to Deal with Gaslighting - Healthline https://www.healthline.com/health/how-to-deal-with-gaslighting

10 Ways to Talk to Someone with Narcissistic Tendencies https://psychcentral.com/disorders/how-to-talk-to-someone-with-narcissistic-tendencies

How to Protect Yourself When Divorcing a Narcissist https://jacobsberger.com/how-to-protect-yourself-when-divorcing-narcissist/

Co-Parenting With a Toxic Ex: 10 Tips From a Therapist https://www.choosingtherapy.com/co-parenting-with-a-toxic-ex/

Helping Children Cope With a Narcissistic Parent https://www.psychologytoday.com/us/blog/living-on-automatic/202301/helping-children-cope-with-a-narcissistic-parent

The Grey Rock Method: A Technique for Handling Toxic ... https://psychcentral.com/health/grey-rock-method

The Best Co-Parenting Apps – 2023 Update https://www.berkshire-law.com/2023/07/25/the-best-co-parenting-apps-2023-update/

12 Ways to Document and Protect Yourself & Kids in a ... https://lifesavingdivorce.com/document/

How to Spot the Signs of Abusive Texts & Get Help https://www.joinonelove.org/learn/how-to-spot-the-signs-of-abusive-texts-get-help/

10 Ways to Talk to Someone with Narcissistic Tendencies https://psychcentral.com/disorders/how-to-talk-to-someone-with-narcissistic-tendencies

Your Legal Guide to Divorcing a Narcissist https://bartonfamilylaw.com.au/narcissistic-abuse-narcissistic-abuse-personality-disorder/

Co-Parenting With a Narcissist: Challenges and Solutions https://denverfamilycounselingservices.com/co-parenting-with-a-narcissist/

Setting Healthy Boundaries in Relationships https://www.helpguide.org/articles/relationships-communication/setting-healthy-boundaries-in-relationships.htm

8 Family Manipulation Tactics and How to Respond to Them https://www.healthline.com/health/mental-health/family-manipulation

How to communicate effectively with your young child - UNICEF https://www.unicef.org/parenting/child-care/9-tips-for-better-communication

About Parental Alienation | My Site - Dr. Amy Baker https://www.amyjlbaker.com/about-parental-alienation#:

Building Resilience in Children of Divorce https://www.divorcestrategiesnw.com/2019/10/building-resilience-in-children-of-divorce/

Stages of Healing After Narcissistic Abuse - Choosing Therapy https://www.choosingtherapy.com/stages-of-healing-after-narcissistic-abuse/

Stress effects on the body https://www.apa.org/topics/stress/body

How to Practice Mindfulness for Emotional Resilience https://www.additudemag.com/how-to-practice-mindfulness-stress-reduction-adhd/

15 Tips for Setting Boundaries With a Narcissist https://www.choosingtherapy.com/setting-boundaries-with-a-narcissist/

Financial Independence After Divorce: You Can Go Your ... https://www.kiplinger.com/personal-finance/604834/financial-independence-after-divorce-you-can-go-your-own-way

How To Litigate For Child Support With A Narcissist https://www.forbes.com/sites/patriciafersch/2021/05/20/how-to-litigate-for-child-support-with-a-narcissist/

child custody | Wex | US Law | LII / Legal Information Institute https://www.law.cornell.edu/wex/child_custody

Documentation in Child Custody Cases https://alimentor.org/en/articles/documentation-in-child-custody-cases.html

8 Steps to Reclaiming Your Authentic Self After Divorce https://movingpastdivorce.com/8-steps-to-reclaiming-your-authentic-self-after-divorce/

Moving On: How To Set Goals After Breakup Or Divorce https://www.breakupandshine.com/2019/09/07/divorce-goals/

How to Let Go: 12 Tips for Letting Go of the Past - Healthline https://www.healthline.com/health/how-to-let-go

Co-Parenting with a Narcissist: Tips for Making It Work https://www.healthline.com/health/parenting/co-parenting-with-a-narcissist

How the Grey Rock Method Works https://health.clevelandclinic.org/grey-rock-method

A Guide to Building a Case Against a Narcissistic Ex https://www.joleenalouislaw.com/blog/a-guide-to-building-a-case-against-a-narcissistic-ex

Everything You Need to Know about Detached Mindfulness https://metacognitivetherapycentral.com/everything-you-need-to-know-about-detached-mindfulness/

How to End a Smear Campaign by Narcissist https://rexxfield.com/smear-campaign-by-narcissist/

15 Tips for Setting Boundaries With a Narcissist https://www.choosingtherapy.com/setting-boundaries-with-a-narcissist/

Children of High-Conflict Divorce Face Many Challenges https://www.psychiatrictimes.com/view/children-high-conflict-divorce-face-many-challenges

How to start and run an effective co-parent support group http://sfhelp.org/sf/help/group.htm

The Impact of Growing up with a Narcissistic Parent https://www.heatherhayes.com/the-impact-of-growing-up-with-a-narcissistic-parent/

Images "Designed by Freepik" www.freepik.com

www.ingramcontent.com/pod-product-compliance
Lightning Source LLC
Chambersburg PA
CBHW052139070526
44585CB00017B/1896